Black London

BLACK
LONDON

Avril Nanton &
Jody Burton

inkspire

First published in Great Britain in 2021 by Inkspire

Inkspire is an imprint of Fox Chapel Publishers International Ltd.
3 The Bridle Way, Selsey, Chichester, PO20 0RS

Project Team
Publisher: Helen Brocklehurst
Designer: Tom Whitlock
Editor: Nick Fawcett
Proofreader: Katie Stockermans
Maps: Lovell Johns

ISBN 978-1-913-61819-3

A CIP catalogue record for this book is available from The British Library

Printed and bound in Great Britain

10 9 8 7 6 5 4 3

Cover design: Tom Whitlock

The paper used within this book is from
well-managed forests and other responsible sources.

Standing on giants' shoulders

CONTENTS

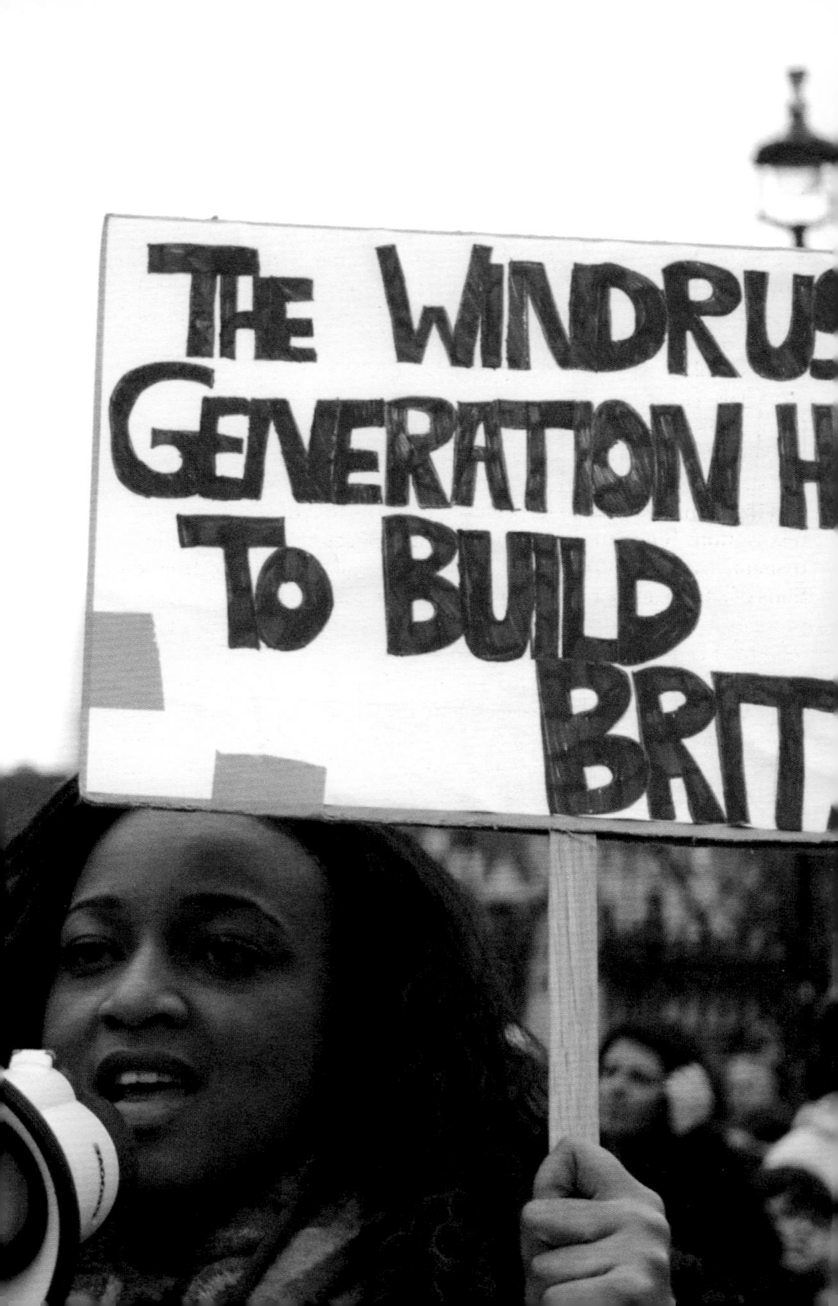
THE WINDRUS
GENERATION H
TO BUILD
BRIT

WELCOME TO BLACK LONDON

London has a rich multicultural history of which we should all be proud. Historically, black people have been here for a very long time. Royal 'blacke trumpeter' John Blanke, for example, arrived in Britain as part of the entourage of Katherine of Aragon in the early years of the sixteenth century.

This book is a historical guide to black global history in London, as well as a compendium of information about things to see, from Cleopatra's Needle dating as far back as 1460 BCE, to the Black Lives Matter mural painted in Woolwich in 2020, which celebrates familiar heroes such as Mary Seacole, Ignatius Sancho and Marcus Garvey, and highlights other people, places and events that deserve wider recognition. There are also stories in these pages of black and white resistance and the struggle for freedom and equality, ranging from the Sons of Africa and Granville Sharp in the sixteenth century, to race protests in the twentieth century. Learn the stories behind the plaques, monuments, murals, statues and artworks.

London's role as a Roman colony and Britain's later role in world trade enslavement during its Empire period have, in turn, made the UK a diverse land and London a global city. These connected histories are reflected in the city's place names, statues and other historical artefacts and landmarks, illustrating the diversity of an all too rarely told British history that stretches back long before the arrival of the ship *HMT* (His Majesty's Transport) *Empire Windrush* in 1948. Windrush is an important chapter in black Britain's history and heritage. It marks the commencement of modern black Britain.

To cover this vibrant history, we have arranged the key London boroughs into five areas. Some are particularly rich in black history and others less so. Evidence of the black presence is particularly abundant in central London, the East End, Brixton, Tottenham and Notting Hill. Each of these neighbourhoods has a particular history, links to the black community and layers to the past. Ultimately, the landmarks, people and places you will read about here demonstrate the significant black contribution in shaping London's history.

HISTORY OF THE SHIP *HMT EMPIRE WINDRUSH*

In 1930 the Motor Vessel *Monte Rosa* was launched as a passenger liner and cruise ship in Germany. Owned and operated by the German shipping line Hamburg Süd, she was used during the Second World War as a troopship by the German navy. Subsequently, the British took the ship as a prize for defeating the Germans. They decided to name it the *Empire Windrush* and continued to use it as a troopship. Operated for the British government by the New Zealand Shipping Company, the ship docked at Kingston, Jamaica, on 24 May 1948 only to pick up servicemen who were on leave, but people from all over the Caribbean had heard about its arrival and many had purchased tickets to England. Having heard so much about the UK, they wanted to see what the Mother Country looked like, so by the time the ship left Jamaica it was packed not only with returning servicemen but with citizens (the British Nationality Act 1948, according citizenship to all British subjects with links to the United Kingdom or a British colony, was going through Parliament at the time) who were curious, seeking adventure and looking for work.

The ship finally arrived in the UK on 21 June 1948, docking at Tilbury, but the passengers were not allowed to disembark until the next day as it was so late. Of the 1,027 onboard, 802 gave the Caribbean as their last place of residence, although the official figure was recorded as 492. The majority of passengers were men. Eighty-six were children aged 12 and under.

Nearly 16 years later, in what proved to be the final journey of the *HMT Empire Windrush*, an explosion and fierce fire in the engine room killed four crew members as the ship was travelling from Hong Kong to Britain in 1954. The ship sank but the remaining crew and passengers were all rescued.

LONDON PLAQUES

Plaques serve as important historical markers. They are permanent signs in public places commemorating noteworthy people, organisations and events linked to that location. The sites generally relate to a birthplace, residence, workplace or occasionally place of death. The signs can be made of ceramic, stone, metal or other materials.

Familiar to most will be the celebrated blue plaque scheme - the oldest plaque system in the world - inaugurated by the Society of Arts in 1867. After subsequently being administered by the London County Council and then Greater London Council, responsibility for the scheme was taken on by English Heritage in 1986. An important criterion for English Heritage, which oversees the scheme via a committee, is that the nominated person must have been dead for at least 20 years. In 2016 the organisation launched a diversity initiative to address the lack of plaques commemorating those from an African Caribbean and Asian heritage. Two black male trustees joined the charity's board in 2018: Kunle Olulode, director of Voice4Change and a national advocate for the black and minority ethnic voluntary and community sector; and David Olusoga, historian, broadcaster and film-maker.

Most London boroughs have their own schemes and many are voted for by the public. Their plaques come in a variety of colours, blue being the predominate choice, but also including green in Islington and brown in Camden and Hackney. Unlike those of English Heritage, Southwark Heritage Association's plaques - which are also blue - commemorate living people.

Since 2004, the Nubian Jak Community Trust, headed by Jak Beula, has recognised the contribution of important black figures and raised the awareness of black history in Britain through its commemorative plaque and sculpture scheme. The trust works in collaboration with local boroughs and organisations, its plaques recognising past and living people as well as events.

In 2016 historian David Olusoga presented *A Forgotten History*, part of the BBC's Black and British season that highlighted local and global black history. A number of Black History Project plaques were unveiled in London, elsewhere in the UK and across former British colonies and the Commonwealth.

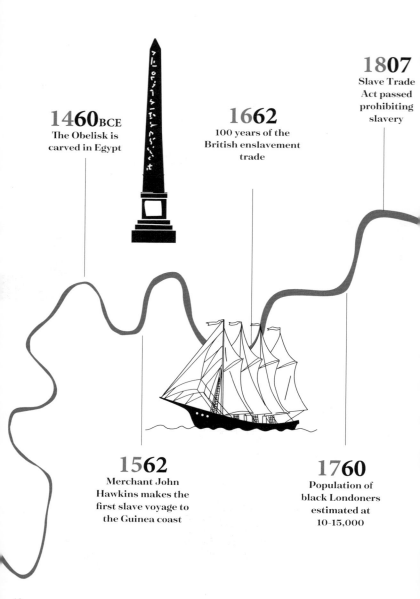

1807
Slave Trade
Act passed
prohibiting
slavery

1460BCE
The Obelisk is
carved in Egypt

1662
100 years of the
British enslavement
trade

1562
Merchant John
Hawkins makes the
first slave voyage to
the Guinea coast

1760
Population of
black Londoners
estimated at
10-15,000

1987
First three black
Members of
Parliament

2020
Black Lives Matter
protests take place
globally during the
COVID-19 pandemic

1948
HMT Empire Windrush
arrives at Tilbury
Docks

1962
Jamaica gains its
independence from
Britain

1914/39
2 million African and
Caribbean service
personnel participate in
both world wars

2007
200 years of
emancipation

TIMELINE

Before the Common Era (BCE)

1460
BCE
– The Obelisk is carved in Egypt. In 1878 it is moved to London's Victoria Embankment, flanked by two faux sphinxes. It becomes known as 'Cleopatra's Needle'.

Enlightenment

1492 – Christopher Columbus lands in the Caribbean. Britain and Europe wage a continuous battle for control and colonisation of these lands. The native Amerindian population, including the Taino, Arawaks and Caribs, is virtually annihilated. However, some native people still survive in the Caribbean. Dominica has a territory inhabited by the Kalinago – formerly known as Carib Indians – and the Jamaican Coat of Arms depicts a male and female Taino.

Tudor

1511 – John Blanke is a court trumpeter to King Henry VII and Henry VIII.

1562 – Merchant John Hawkins makes the first slave voyage to the Guinea coast, in Africa, sponsored by Queen Elizabeth I.

1578 – England grants Sir Humphrey Gilbert a patent to explore and colonise North America.

1579 – English navigator Francis Drake lands on the coast of California at Drakes Bay, and names it 'New Albion'.

1587 – Walter Raleigh names land in North America 'Virginia' in honour of Elizabeth I, the Virgin Queen.

1601 – Queen Elizabeth I issues a proclamation ordering the expulsion of black settlers from England.

Stuart

1604	– *Othello*, by William Shakespeare, is first performed.
1619	– The first enslaved African is taken to the British colony of Virginia, USA. The 13 British colonies are established using African enslaved labour. The country's native American Indians are decimated and forced out on to reservations.
1655	– Britain claims Jamaica from the Spanish. It establishes a settlement and develops its lucrative sugar plantations.
1660	– The Royal African Company is formed by the Crown and London merchants to exploit gold fields in Africa. It also monopolises slavery in the Gold Coast and goes on to ship more African people to the Americas than any other institution in the history of the Atlantic enslavement era.
1662	100 years of the British enslavement trade.
1698 -1720	– London becomes the leading slave port in Britain, followed by Bristol and Liverpool.

Georgian

1714	– During the Georgian period numerous British newspapers advertise 'runaways and rewards' for black slaves who were bought and sold in England.
1730	– First Maroon uprising in Jamaica.
1760	– Population of black Londoners estimated at between 10,000 and 15,000, including servants, slaves, seamen, and free men and women. – Slave revolts and uprisings in Jamaica (Tacky's War).
1762	200 years of the British enslavement trade.
1772	– Lord Mansfield judges the Somerset case and rules against enforced removal of black individuals from the UK.
1775 -83	– American War of Independence: some states revolt against British rule. Free black men and slaves fight on both sides.

1780	– The anti-Catholic Gordon Riots occur in London. Rioters include some identified as 'black' or 'mulatto' (white and black).
	– The London Society of West India Planters and Merchants is founded. The organisation of British sugar merchants, absentee planters and colonial agents was instrumental in resisting the abolition of slavery and maintaining a plantocracy.
1781	– Lord Mansfield judges the Zong case in which 133 live slaves were thrown overboard from a British ship. Insurance claims for loss of 'property' were filed.
1783	– Following Britain's defeat in the American war of Independence, thousands of 'black loyalists' who fought on the side of the British arrive in London but are denied pensions and face poverty.
1789	– In France, the monarchy is overthrown. This leads to revolution in Haiti.
1791	– Slave uprising in St Domingue (Haiti), led by the black general Toussaint L'Ouverture.

Victorian

1802	– The West India Docks are opened at the Isle of Dogs. Built by the West India Dock Company for trade with the West Indies in tobacco, rice, wine, brandy and rum.
1807	– Slave Trade Act 1807 passed. This act only prohibited the slave trade; it did not stop it. The acts of slavery continued until 1833 when the Slavery Abolition Act made the purchase and ownership of enslaved people illegal within the British Empire.
1820	– Cato Street Conspiracy. A small group of radicals plotted to assassinate the prime minister and members of the British cabinet. They include William Davidson, the son of the Jamaican attorney general and a black female. He and four other conspirators were tried, hanged and decapitated.

1831	– Major slave revolt led by Samuel Sharpe in Jamaica. – Nat Turner leads a slave revolt in Virginia, USA. He is caught and executed along with 18 others.
1833	– Slavery Abolition Act. Although slavery is abolished throughout the British Empire, it is replaced by an enforced 'apprenticeship' of six years. The British government paid slave owners compensation for the loss of their slaves.
1834	– Britain begins recruiting indentured labour, mainly from India and China, to work on Caribbean plantations.
1838	– The British Parliament ends the 'apprenticeship' system. Enslaved people become free on 1 August in theory. However, in practice there was no economic freedom, equality or suffrage. Newly freed people refused to work for low wages but had scant alternatives. – Britain maintains control in all areas - including political, economic, legislation, land and resources - in Africa and the Caribbean. This also includes the imposition of a British educational system and a hierarchy of divide and rule based on colour, class and religion.
1857	– The Dred Scott decision in America makes slavery legal all over the USA.
1859	– The last known slave ship, *Clotilda*, arrives in the USA carrying between 110 and 160 enslaved people.
1865	– The Morant Bay Rebellion in Jamaica is led by Paul Bogle. – Slavery is officially abolished in the USA.
1884 -85	– Congress of Berlin: Britain and several European countries plan the partition and control of Africa.
1897	– A collection of over a thousand bronzes known as the Benin bronzes is looted by British forces from the royal palace of the Kingdom of Benin.

20th century

1900	– First Pan-African Conference held in London: delegates petition Queen Victoria to investigate the treatment of Africans in South Africa and Rhodesia.

1907	100 years of emancipation.
1914 -18	– The First World War: soldiers from Africa, Asia and the Caribbean volunteer and enlist. Black sailors and a small number of African and Caribbean students also serve as merchant seamen.
1919	– Race riots in London and other UK cities.
1924	– King Tutankhamun's tomb is opened by Howard Carter.
1924 -25	– British Empire Exhibition is held at Wembley.
1931	– Dr Harold Moody forms the League of Coloured Peoples.
1936	– African American athlete Jesse Owens wins four gold medals at the Berlin Olympics, witnessed by Hitler.
1938	100 years of British colonial rule.
1939 -45	– The Second World War: soldiers from Africa, Asia and the Caribbean volunteer and enlist.
1941	– Ken 'Snakehips' Johnson is killed, aged 26, at the Café de Paris, London, during a German air raid. He was the leader of a West Indian swing band and a regular on BBC radio.
1944	– Jamaica gains universal adult suffrage (voting rights).
1948	– *HMT Empire Windrush* arrives at Tilbury Docks. Of the 1,027 passengers, 492 come from the Caribbean. The Trinidadian calypsonian stage-named Lord Kitchener was interviewed at the dock and sang 'London is the Place for Me'. – The NHS is founded.
1955	– Rosa Parks is arrested for sitting in the white section of a segregated bus in Alabama, USA.
1957	– Ghana (formerly the Gold Coast) is the first African country to gain independence from Britain. – Winifred Atwell becomes the first black woman to have a number one record in the UK, selling over one million copies.

1958
- The Notting Hill uprisings break out after white youth attacks on black people.
- Claudia Jones founds the *West Indian Gazette* newspaper.

1959
- The precursor to the Notting Hill Carnival is established but is known simply as a Caribbean carnival.

1960
- The Sharpeville Massacre in South Africa.

1962
- Jamaica gains its independence from Britain. Its national motto, 'Out of Many, One People', represents the population's multiracial roots.
- The Commonwealth Immigrants Act restricts black entry to Britain.

1963
- Doctor Martin Luther King delivers his 'Let freedom ring' also known as the 'I have a dream' speech at the civil rights march on Washington, DC.
- Paul Stephenson leads the Bristol Bus Boycott after the bus company refuses to employ black and Asian people.
- Jomo Kenyatta becomes the first black prime minister of Kenya.

1964
- The Africa Centre opens in London, Covent Garden.
- Dame Jocelyn Barrow and David Pitt are among activists attending a meeting with Martin Luther King, who made a short visit to London en route to Norway to receive the Nobel Peace Prize. They help to establish an umbrella group of associations under The Campaign Against Racial Discrimination (CARD). The organisation lobbied for legislation outlawing discrimination in all areas including housing and employment. It challenged the colour bar against black people working in Oxford Street and various well-known streets such as Carnaby Street.
- Cassius Clay, the boxer, renames himself Muhammad Ali.
- Jamaican singer Millie Small gets to number two in the UK and USA with her single 'My Boy Lollipop' - the first record to popularise Ska music.

1965
- Martin Luther King leads the Montgomery marchers over the Edmund Pettus Bridge in Selma, Alabama.
- Malcolm X is assassinated.

1966	– The New Beacon Bookshop opens in Finsbury Park the first black bookshop in the UK.
1967	– Norwell Roberts from Anguilla becomes the first black policeman to join the London Metropolitan Police. He served for 30 years and was awarded the Queen's Police Medal in 1996.
1968	– Bogle-L'Ouverture Publications is founded by Eric and Jessica Huntley.
	– Martin Luther King is assassinated at the Lorraine Motel, Alabama.
	– Student protests start at Columbia University, USA, creating a wave of student activism that spreads across the globe, including Paris and Mexico.
	– Students also riot in Jamaica in support of political activist Walter Rodney.
	– A Black Power protest is staged at the Olympics in Mexico. Two black American athletes give a raised-fist salute on the winner's podium in support of the Civil Rights Movement. It becomes an iconic image.
1973	– Sybil Phoenix becomes the first black MBE in recognition of her community work, particularly with young women.
1976	– Notting Hill Carnival riots in north-west London.
	– Soweto Massacre in South Africa.
1977	– The Battle of Lewisham. The right-wing National Front party is prevented from marching through New Cross.
	– The American slavery serial *Roots*, based on Alex Haley's book, is aired on British TV.
1978	– Viv Anderson becomes the first black British footballer to play for England.
	– Some 100,000 people take part in a Rock Against Racism march from Trafalgar Square to Victoria Park in Hackney, where an anti-racist concert is staged, featuring both rock and reggae music and musicians.
1979	– Professor Dame Elizabeth Nneka Anionwu helps to establish in Brent the first nurse-led UK Sickle Cell & Thalassaemia Screening and Counselling Centre.

1981	– Brixton riots are followed by the Scarman Report, which concludes that the police force is 'institutionally racist'.
	– The Black Cultural Archives is founded in Brixton.
	– The New Cross fire breaks out, in which 13 young black people die.
	– Black Peoples Day of Action. Around 20,000 people march in reaction to the public and media response to the New Cross fire.
1982	– *The Voice*, a British national black weekly newspaper, is founded. Distribution goes monthly in 2019.
1985	– Riots ignite in Tottenham after Cynthia Jarrett is killed by police.
1987	– Three black MPs (Labour) make history by becoming the first to enter the previously all-white House of Commons, including the first black female MP, Diane Abbott.
	– Black History Month is established in Britain.
1990	– Nelson Mandela is released from prison
1992	– South Africa votes to end apartheid.
1993	– Teenager Stephen Lawrence is murdered in Eltham, south-east London.
1994	– The Stuart Hall Library is opened.
1996	– Nelson Mandela visits Brixton. He also meets the Lawrence family.
	– The MOBO Awards are launched. The first black awards show in Europe, it represented music (of black origin) and urban culture.
	– Operation Black Vote is launched.

21st century

| 2000 | – The BBC series *Millennium* is shown and includes the history of the fourteenth-century ruler Mansa Musa, from Mali, reputedly the richest ever person in history. |
| | – Labour MP for Haringey, Bernie Grant, dies of a heart attack and is replaced by David Lammy MP. |

2004 — Andrea Levy's book *Small Island* is published; it is later adapted by the BBC and staged at the National Theatre. Levy died in 2019 and her archive of work was acquired by The British Library.

2005 — The first Annual Huntley Conference is held.
— Frank Bowling becomes the first black artist to be elected to the Royal Academy of Art.
— John Sentamu is named Bishop of York. Born in Uganda, he is the first black bishop in the UK.

2006 — UK Black Pride Day is established by Phyllis Akua Opoku-Gyimah, aka Lady Phyll, to celebrate black LGBTQ+ people.
— Ellen Johnson Sirleaf is sworn in as Liberia's new president. She becomes Africa's first female elected head of state.

2007 — 200 years of emancipation.

2009 — International Nelson Mandela Day is established.
— Barack Obama becomes the first black president of the United States.
— Michelle Obama visits an Islington school.

2011 — Riots commence in Tottenham after Mark Duggan is murdered by police. They spread throughout London and the rest of the UK.

2012 — London Olympic winners include Team GB's first female boxer Nicola Adams, runner Mo Farah and heptathlon champion Jessica Ennis.
— Trayvon Martin, aged 17, is murdered by George Zimmerman in the USA. Zimmerman is acquitted of his murder and released.

2013 — The protest movement Black Lives Matter is founded in the USA and becomes the Black Lives Matter Global Network in the same year.

2014 — A jury decides in the Mark Duggan case that he was killed lawfully by the police.
— Lewis Hamilton wins the 2014 Japanese Grand Prix. He goes on to win the Formula 1 World Title later in the year. In 2020 he receives an MBE and is awarded Sports Personality of the Year by the BBC.

2015	– Chi-chi Nwanoku founds Chineke, Europe's first majority black and minority ethnic orchestra.

2015
- Chi-chi Nwanoku founds Chineke, Europe's first majority black and minority ethnic orchestra.
- Prime Minister David Cameron visits Jamaica, but, rather than offering reparations, he provides funds to build more jails, which causes a furore.
- Loans taken out by the British government to compensate slave owners in 1833 are finally repaid.

2017
- London Bridge is attacked by terrorists. Black PC Wayne Marques helps to save lives.
- Edward Enninful becomes the first black editor of *British Vogue* magazine.
- The Jhalak Prize is established to celebrate British black and Asian writers.
- Reni Eddo-Lodge's book *Why I'm No Longer Talking to White People About Race* is published. It wins the Jhalak Prize in 2018.
- The first Diaspora Pavilion exhibition, at the 57th Venice Biennale, showcases the work of 19 established and emerging black artists. They include *The British Library* by Yinka Shonibare MBE and a photography collection entitled *Dwelling: In This Space We Breathe*, by Khadija Saye.
- Fire ravages through Grenfell Tower, a block of flats in the Royal Borough of Kensington and Chelsea. Seventy-two people are killed, most of them black and minority ethnic. Artist Khadija Saye and her mother, Mary Ajaoi Augustus Mendy, are among the victims.

2018
- Amber Rudd resigns as Home Secretary following the Windrush Scandal.
- Meghan Markel marries Prince Harry in Windsor. An estimated 1.9 billion people watch the wedding, which includes performances from cellist Sheku Kanneh-Mason and The Kingdom Choir. By 2020, the pair relinquish their royal titles and leave the UK to set up home in the USA.

2019
- First year of the Stephen Lawrence Day.
- First year of Windrush Day (see p. 26).
- Bernardine Evaristo, MBE, wins the Booker Prize with *Girl, Woman, Other*, which featured as one of Barack Obama's favourite books of the year.

2020
- Coronavirus pandemic: Baroness Doreen Lawrence appointed as Labour's race relations adviser. She leads a review into the high impact of coronavirus on BAME communities.
- Visionary Honours Awards: winners include George the Poet, the film *Blue Story* and song *Black* by Dave.
- George Floyd is murdered by police in the USA. Protests under the umbrella group Black Lives Matter Global Network (BLM) take place across America. Despite the coronavirus restrictions, demonstrations and marches in solidarity occur globally, including the UK.
- During BLM protests in Bristol, the statue of slave owner Edward Colston is toppled.
- In London, Winston Churchill's statue is daubed with the words 'was a racist.'
- The statue of another slave owner, Robert Milligan, is removed from the front of the Museum of London Docklands.
- Two black British female authors, Bernardine Evaristo and Reni Eddo-Lodge, top the fiction and non-fiction book charts.
- Manchester United striker Marcus Rashford successfully challenges the government to support free school meals for families in need. He receives an MBE in 2021.
- Premier League football restarts with a minute's silence for COVID-19 victims; players wear sport shirts emblazoned with BLM and take the knee in support of racial equality.
- Artists Thomas J. Price and Veronica Ryan are commissioned to create the first permanent public sculptures to honour the Windrush generation in the UK. The works are scheduled to be unveiled in the borough of Hackney in 2021.
- The London Mayor sets up the Commission for Diversity in the Public Realm.
- A BLM mural is unveiled in Woolwich.

Huntley Conference
February (first week)

The archives of Guyanese-born political activists Jessica Huntley and Eric Huntley are held at the London Metropolitan Archives in East London. Started in 2005, the Annual Huntley Conference is organised by the charity Friends of the Huntley Archives (FHALMA).

Stephen Lawrence Day
22 April

The first annual national commemoration of Stephen took place in 2019. He was only 18 years old when he was murdered by white racists in 1993. The Stephen Lawrence Charitable Trust launched an architect's competition in 2019 to design an 18-mile marker for the London Marathon (held each March) dedicated to his life.

Windrush Day
22 June

The year 2019 saw the first annual celebration of Windrush Day, celebrating the first modern day mass immigration from the Caribbean islands. The day recognises the contribution of the Windrush generation. Government plans for a Windrush memorial are under discussion, and in 2021 Hackney Council plans to unveil a major artwork to honour the local Windrush community.

UK Black Pride
First Sunday of July

UK Black Pride is Europe's largest celebration for Lesbian, Gay, Bisexual, Transgender and Queer (LGBTQ+) people of African, Asian, Caribbean, Middle Eastern and Latin American descent. First celebrated in 2006, the event is part of the annual celebrations of Pride month.

Nelson Mandela Day
18 July

This day was officially declared by the United Nations in November 2009, with the first Mandela Day held on 18 July 2010, the date of his birthday. It is now an annual international day in his honour.

Sankofa Day (International Day for the Remembrance of the Slave Trade and its Abolition)
23 August

In 1998 the United Nations Educational, Scientific and Cultural Organisation (UNESCO), designated this date as the International Day for the Remembrance of the Slave Trade and its Abolition, and from 2016 onwards, victims of the trade have been remembered and honoured on Sankofa Day in a ceremony at London's Trafalgar Square. Symbolised by a bird with its head turned backwards to take an egg from its back, the word sankofa means learning from the past to build the future.

Notting Hill Carnival
Last Sunday and Bank Holiday Monday of August

This carnival started in 1959 as a community festival and is now the largest in Europe. It is a celebration of African Caribbean culture and tradition via music, masquerade and food.

Black History Month
October

Founded in 1987 under the Greater London Council (GLC), this national celebration aims to promote and celebrate black British contributions to society, and to foster an understanding of black history through educational and cultural events.

Tottenham Literary Festival
November

Established in 2019, the Tottenham Literature Festival is an annual nine-day event. It is held at the Bernie Grant Arts Centre, and aims to highlight work by black writers and to champion diverse children's literature.

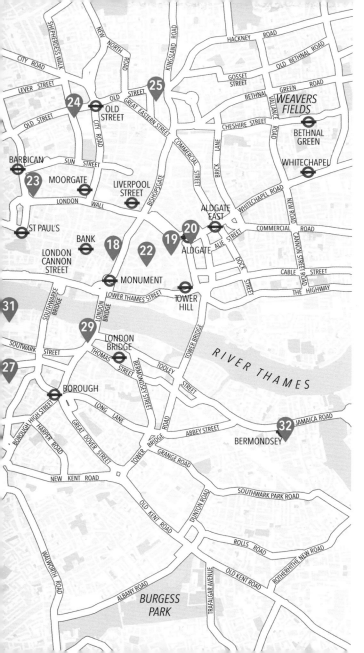

1. CLEOPATRA'S NEEDLE
2. IGNATIUS SANCHO
3. OLAUDAH EQUIANO
4. 37 TOTTENHAM STREET
5. OTTOBAH CUGOANO
6. BILL RICHMOND
7. GEORGE RYAN
8. JOHNSON BEHARRY
9. 14 SOHO SQUARE
10. BUXTON MEMORIAL FOUNTAIN
11. JOMO KENYATTA
12. RONALD MOODY
13. NELSON MANDELA
14. JIMI HENDRIX

15. STUART HALL
16. MODERN MARTYRS
17. MEMORIAL GATES
18. JAMAICA WINE HOUSE
19. FRANCES BARBER
20. PHILLIS WHEATLEY
21. JONATHAN STRONG & GRANVILLE SHARP
22. GILT OF CAIN
23. MUSEUM OF LONDON
24. NETWORK
25. AUTOGRAPH GALLERY
26. ERIC & JESSICA HUNTLEY
27. THE BLACK FRIAR
28. THE AFRICA CENTRE

29. WAYNE MARQUES
30. MARY SEACOLE
31. THE BRITISH LIBRARY
32. JAMAICA ROAD
33. ROBERT WEDDERBURN
34. MAYA ANGELOU
35. BENIN BRONZES
36. THE PETRIE MUSEUM OF EGYPTIAN ARCHAEOLOGY
37. MARY PRINCE
38. YMCA CLUB
39. AFRICAN NATIONAL CONGRESS
40. SIDNEY BECHET

1

CENTRAL AND EAST LONDON

The boroughs of Westminster, the City and Tower Hamlets have always had their fair share of Africans and Caribbeans living in them. From the St Giles area in Covent Garden where many poor people lived, including black people, to Whitehall where Ignatius Sancho had a grocery shop and became the first black man to vote in Britain, the centre of London is rich with Black landmarks. The City has a rather dubious link with Africa and the Caribbean. City merchants were all rich men and women some of whose money came from the enslavement trade, many of them having plantations in the Americas and the Caribbean.

The east end of London was alive with sailors coming from afar. Due to the proximity of the Thames, Black and Asian sailors stayed at the Strangers' Home for Asiatics, Africans and South Sea Islanders. From there they would meet others of their ilk and bring each other up to date with the latest news from home. People like George Ryan may have found solace there when they arrived in London. Over the last 100 years the East End, the Docklands area in particular, has been regenerated. The area also now houses the 'London Sugar and Slavery' permanent exhibition at the Museum of London Docklands.

CLEOPATRA'S NEEDLE

LANDMARK (1460 BCE)

Westminster Embankment,
WC2N 6PB

Cleopatra's Needle (aka the obelisk) is over 3,500 years old. It was fashioned during the reign of Pharaoh Thutmose III and stood in Heliopolis (modern-day Cairo). The monument was presented to the British in 1819 by the then ruler of Egypt, Muhammad Ali, but remained in situ for another 70 years. In 1878 it was finally shipped to London by Sir William Erasmus Wilson, an anatomist and dermatologist.

The journey was perilous and six men lost their lives, but when it finally arrived in London, it was placed on the Embankment, where John Vulliamy cast supports in bronze and two sphinxes to watch over it. Several canopic jars were placed inside containing items of the day as future memorials. The story of how the monument arrived is inscribed on the base on four bronze relief panels. Nearby benches are supported by elaborate winged sphinxes, and the hieroglyphics on the monument reveal how advanced the Egyptians' knowledge of science and maths was at a time when most cultures had little grasp of such matters.

IGNATIUS SANCHO

COMPOSER, AUTHOR, ACTOR, ABOLITIONIST (1729-80)

Foreign and Commonwealth Office, King Charles Street, SW1A 2AH

The Nubian Jak plaque shown here was erected in 2007 to commemorate Ignatius Sancho's life. It is situated in the street where he later owned a grocery shop.

Sancho was born in c.1729 on a slave ship en route to the West Indies from West Africa. His mother died when he was born and his father committed suicide rather than live in enslavement. By the time he was two years old, Ignatius was taken to live in Greenwich, London, where he spent the first period of his life working as a servant for three sisters. He did not like the sisters but, having nowhere else to go, he remained with them for 18 years. While there, he met the Duke of Montagu, who took a shine to him. Sancho ran away to live with the Duke and there he learnt to read and write. A memorial plaque can also be seen at the remains of Montagu House in Greenwich Park.

In 1758 Sancho married Anne Osborne, a black woman with whom he had seven children. After the duke died, leaving Sancho an inheritance, he left the household and set up a grocery shop in King Charles Street. As a financially independent male, and a property holder, he was eligible to vote, and in 1774 he became the first African to vote in a British general election.

During his lifetime Sancho wrote letters, composed music, acted on stage, and was an abolitionist. He was painted by Gainsborough, making him one of the few black men to have his portrait painted by a famous artist. His image featured in 2007 on a Royal Mail commemorative stamp marking 200 years since the abolition of the slave trade. Sancho voted again in 1780 just before his death in the same year. His obituary in *The Times* was the first one published for an African in a British newspaper. After he died, many of his letters were found by his son and published in a book called *The Letters of the late Ignatius Sancho, an African* in 1781.

OLAUDAH EQUIANO
SLAVE, ABOLITIONIST AND AUTHOR (1745-97)
67–73 Riding House Street, Fitzrovia, W1W 7EJ

Olaudah Equiano was born in 1745 in Eastern Nigeria. Captured as a child and shipped into slavery, his journey took him to America, where he was sold to Captain Pascal, who renamed him Gustavus Vassa after a Swedish king, and took him on naval service. When Pascal visited London in 1759, Equiano stayed in Greenwich and was baptised in Westminster. He believed his years of naval service and baptism had earned him his freedom, but in 1762 he was kidnapped at Deptford and resold into slavery. On the merchant ships, Equiano worked as a deckhand, valet and barber. He subsequently learnt to read and write – these skills enabled him to trade a little on the side, selling fruits and trinkets and finally earning enough money to purchase his freedom.

In 1767 he settled in London, where he worked closely with Granville Sharp in the anti-slavery movement, alerting him in 1781 to the scandal of the Zong slave ship, from which slaves were thrown overboard when the ship ran into difficulty, an insurance claim subsequently being filed for their loss. Equiano was a prominent member of the 'Sons of Africa', a group of black free men in London, including abolitionist, political activist and philosopher Ottobah Cugoano, who used their experiences and voices to lobby Parliament and campaign for abolition.

Equiano published his autobiography, *The Interesting Narrative of the Life of Olaudah Equiano*, in 1789. He travelled widely promoting it and championing the anti-slavery message. The book became popular nationally and internationally, running to nine editions by 1797, and is still in print to date. In 1792 Equiano married an Englishwoman from Soham, with whom he had two daughters. He died five years later on 31 March 1797.

Olaudah Equiano has multiple commemorations in London. The London Borough plaque shown here was unveiled in October 2000 as part of London's annual Black History Month celebrations. In 2018 Equiano's former residence was included in *Historic England's History of England in 100 Places*, featured under the category 'Power, Protest and Progress'. Like Ignatius Sancho, Equiano also featured in 2007 on one of the Royal Mail stamps commemorating the abolition of the slave trade in 1807. The stamp was designed by Howard Brown, the original portrait – which hangs in the National Portrait Gallery – being painted by W. Denton dating from 1789.

The oval memorial tablet at St Margaret's Church, Westminster, SW1P 3JX, is by the sculptor Marcia Bennett-Male. It was unveiled in 2009 by the Archbishop of York. Equiano was baptised in the church's font in 1759.

37 TOTTENHAM STREET
HOME OF OLAUDAH EQUIANO
37 Tottenham Street, W1T 4RU

I n 2020, The Equiano Society unveiled a blue plaque at this address in Fitzrovia. Equiano lived here in 1788 and wrote part of his autobiography, *The Interesting Narrative of the Life of Olaudah Equiano* (see entry above).

OTTOBAH CUGOANO
ABOLITIONIST, PHILOSOPHER AND AUTHOR (c.1757)
Schomberg House, Pall Mall, SW1Y 5ES

Q uobna Ottobah Cugoano – also known as John Stuart –was born in the Gold Coast of West Africa (Ghana), from where he was captured, sold and taken as a slave to Grenada, where, in 1772, a merchant bought him and took him to England.

Taught to read and write by his owners, and finally granted his freedom after the rulings of the Somerset case in the same year, he found work with artists Richard and Maria Cosway, through whom he became acquainted with several British political and cultural figures. Cugoano joined the Sons of Africa, a group of African abolitionists in Britain that included Olaudah Equiano. In 1787 he published his book *Thoughts and Sentiments on the Evil and Wicked Traffic of the Slavery and Commerce of the Human Species*, in which he called for the abolition of slavery and immediate emancipation of all slaves. He argued that the slave's duty was to escape from slavery, and that force should be used to prevent further enslavement. Cugoano called for the establishment of schools in Britain especially for African students. In 1791 he moved to 12 Queen Street in Mayfair with the Cosways. His last known letter, written in 1791, mentions travelling to 'upwards of fifty places' to promote the book, and notes that he found that 'complexion is a predominant prejudice'. Unfortunately, Cugoano disappears from history after this record and no more is heard about him.

The English Heritage plaque can be found at Schomberg House, Pall Mall, Westminster. It was unveiled in November 2020.

BILL RICHMOND
BOXER (1763–1829)
Tom Cribb Pub, 36 Panton Street, SW1Y 4EA

Bill Richmond, boxer, is one of the few black people to have more than one plaque attributed to them. Both can be seen at the Tom Cribb pub. The BBC History Project plaque was put up outside the pub in 2016 at an event attended by black British historian David Olusoga, boxer Ambrose Mendy, and actor Hugh Quarshie. The second pictorial plaque, which can be viewed inside, was erected by Earl Percy, the current Duke of Northumberland, in 2015.

Richmond was born enslaved in 1763 in New York. He came to Britain in 1777 as a servant to the Earl of Northumberland and was eventually released by him. Although he was a welterweight, he fought bigger, heavier men. His nickname was 'The Black Terror'. One of the most famous fights was between Richmond and Tom Cribb, a white British No. 1 boxer – an encounter that led to Cribb and Richmond becoming lifelong friends. Richmond also befriended another freed boxing slave, Tom Molineaux, who he trained – unsuccessfully as it turned out – to fight for the world boxing championship. Retiring after 20 career contests, Richmond became a gym instructor and trainer, teaching people such as Lord Byron how to box. Like many one-time boxers, in addition to the boxing gym he owned he also bought and ran a pub: the Horse and Dolphin in Leicester Square. Richmond died in London in 1829, aged 66.

GEORGE RYAN
SAILOR (c.1781)
Nelson's Column, Trafalgar Square, WC2

Nelson's Column in Trafalgar Square was designed by William Railton and built in 1843 to commemorate Admiral Horatio Nelson, who died at the Battle of Trafalgar in 1805. The pedestal at the base of the column is decorated with four bronze relief panels, cast from captured French guns. They depict Nelson's most famous battles: St Vincent, Copenhagen, The Nile and his death scene on *The Victory*. This latter panel – The Battle of Trafalgar (facing out towards Whitehall) was created by sculptor John Edward Carew and was the first to be displayed in 1849.

Beneath the image, the words 'England expects every man will do his duty' are inscribed within the frame. On the left of the panel, you can see a sailor of black appearance holding a rifle near to the dying Nelson. The crew list identifies him as 24-year-old 'African'-born George Ryan, although he may, in fact, have been born in Montserrat.

Ryan was part of a multinational crew (many of whom would have been pressed-ganged into service) that came from Britain, India, America, the West Indies, Malta, Italy and Africa. He served in the Royal Navy until 1813 when he was injured and honourably discharged aged 32.

14 SOHO SQUARE
HOME OF MARY SECOLE
14 Soho Square, W1D 3QG

Home of Jamaican nurse Mary Seacole (see p.67). This is the place where she started writing her autobiography and is thought to have still been living here when it was published in July 1857.

JOHNSON BEHARRY
SOLDIER AND BRITISH NATIONAL HERO (b. 1979)
National Portrait Gallery, St Martin's Place, WC2H 0HE

Painted by artist Emma Wesley in 2006, this portrait of soldier and British national hero Johnson Beharry (born in 1979) hangs in the National Portrait Gallery. Beharry was born in Grenada and came to live in England in 1999. He joined the army and served in Northern Ireland, Kosovo and Iraq.

In May 2004 he performed an act of bravery that earned him a citation with an award for valour of the highest order. Beharry was driving a tank in Iraq which had been called to the assistance of some men that had been ambushed. However, on the way there, the tank itself was attacked causing injury to several of the men inside, and damage to the tank's communications system. Beharry was one of the few that hadn't been injured and was able to steer the tank through the ambush and get the wounded out of the tank while still under heavy fire. His actions enabled a clear passage for upcoming tanks.

Then, in June of the same year, once again under enemy fire, and this time seriously injured, he managed to save himself and his crew from imminent danger. Beharry was driving a tank again when they were ambushed. This time a bomb went off in close proximity to his head and face and he received serious shrapnel injuries to his head, face and brain. But the rest of the crew were also seriously injured, and despite his injuries he managed to maneuver the tank out of danger before collapsing. He was rushed to hospital for emergency brain surgery and a year later in March 2005, while he was still in hospital, he received the Victoria Cross, the highest award for bravery in the British army. He was the first person to receive this award in 30 years, the last one had been given in the Falklands war and those were awarded posthumously. He is also one of the first living persons to receive this award since 1965.

In 2008 he attempted to commit suicide by driving his car into a lamp post at 100 miles per hour. He was clearly suffering from PTSD caused by the injuries he had received from the 2004 bomb blast.

In 2011 Beharry was awarded an Honorary Degree of Engineering from the University of Sussex. Recognised by the British establishment and promoted to lance sergeant in 2012, he now has a public relations role in the Household Division of the Queen's Guards. In 2012, as well as carrying the torch for the Olympic Games, he was given the Freedom of the Borough of Southwark, receiving the same for the borough of Hounslow in 2014. His autobiography, *Barefoot Soldier*, was published in 2013.

The Gallery's collection includes notable figures from the past such as Harold Moody (see p. 136) and Nelson Mandela (see p. 44). In 2017 it acquired 'Black is the New Black,' 37 portraits of influential black Britons by Simon Frederick. See also entries for Mary Seacole, p. 67 and Ira Aldridge, p. 181.

BUXTON MEMORIAL FOUNTAIN
MONUMENT (1865)
Victoria Tower Gardens, Millbank, SW1P 3JA

10

This monument was originally erected in the eastern corner of Parliament Square. It was removed in 1940 and moved to its present position in Victoria Tower Gardens in 1957. The fountain – designed by Samuel Sanders Tuelon, and erected by Charles Buxton, MP, who dedicated it to his father Sir Thomas Fowell Buxton and several abolitionists – commemorates the emancipation of slaves in 1834. When Parliament Square was redesigned in 1949, the fountain was removed, and the original plan was to quietly get rid of it. However, there were strong objections – particularly from the Anti-

Slavery Society – and instead the Parliament Square Act of 1949 was amended to require its re-erection in a new site.

The decorated pillars support a brightly coloured enamelled steel spire, and barely a square inch of the elaborately carved granite monument is without fancy flourishes of some kind. Various scenes relating to Africa, made from mosaic tiles, adorn the structure. One depicts the freeing of a slave. The others relate to stories from *Aesop's Fables*, which have moral and ethical points to make.

JOMO KENYATTA
STATESMAN (1894–1978)

87–99 Cambridge Street, Pimlico, SW1V 4PY

J omo Kenyatta was born in east Africa, the son of a Kikuyu farmer. His first name comes from the Kikuyu word for 'burning spear' and his last from the Maasai term for the bead belt that he often wore.

When Kenya became a British crown colony in 1920, the Kikuyu people were dispossessed of their land, which was then restricted for white settlers. Kenyatta became

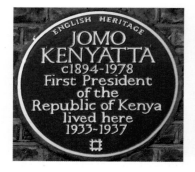

politically active against British colonial rule in his country, acting as the General Secretary of the Kikuyu Central Association, which represented his people's interests and fought for their land rights. Travelling widely, he studied in Moscow and also at the London School of Economics, his thesis evolving into a book, *Facing Mount Kenya* (1938), which highlighted the life of the Kikuyu. In 1945 Kenyatta helped to organise the fifth Pan-African Congress in Manchester, England, which encouraged cooperation between black African nations and demanded independence from colonial rule. He returned to Africa in 1946 as president of the Kenya African Union. In 1953 the Mau Mau rebellions against British colonial rule led to Kenyatta's unjust conviction and imprisonment. Finally, in 1963, Kenya won self-government and Kenyatta was appointed its first prime minister – a post he held until his death in office in 1978. The English Heritage plaque shown here was erected in 2005.

RONALD MOODY
SCULPTOR (1900-84)
Tate Britain, Millbank, SW1P 4RG

It took Ronald Moody a full year to carve *Johanaan* – also referred to as John the Baptist. The figure represents the fusion of universal humanity and was sculpted in Paris in 1936. Purchased by Tate Britain in 1992, it is displayed in the *Walk Through British Art* collection, in the 1930s gallery.

Moody was born in Jamaica, (the younger brother of Harold Moody, see p. 136) and came to England in 1923, initially studying and working in dentistry. However, inspired by visits to the Egyptian and Asian galleries in the British Museum, he decided to become a professional sculptor, going on to exhibit work in the USA, UK and Europe during his long career. He was living in Paris in 1937 where his first one-man exhibition was held, and in 1940 he fled Nazi-occupied France for England. In 1964 he created his famous aluminium sculpture of a stylised bird titled *Savacou*, which referenced Carib-Indian mythology. It was temporarily displayed on the lawn of the Commonwealth Institute in London before being moved permanently to the campus of the University of the West Indies in Jamaica. Moody was part of the Caribbean Artist Movement founded in 1966 by black writers, artists and intellectuals in London. In 1978 he was awarded Jamaica's Musgrave gold medal for contributions to culture. He died in London in 1984.

See also Stephen Lawrence p. 169.

NELSON MANDELA

FREEDOM FIGHTER AND POLITICIAN (1918–2013)

Parliament Square, Westminster, SW1P 3JX

Nelson Rolihlahla Mandela was born in South Africa in 1918 to the Thembu royal family of the Xhosa people. He studied Law at the University of Fort Hare and University of Witwatersrand before working as a lawyer in Johannesburg. In 1943 he joined the African National Congress (ANC) and fought against white minority rule, which oppressed the black majority. Repeatedly arrested for taking part in various anti-apartheid campaigns, in 1964 he was imprisoned for life, going on to serve 27 years of his sentence before being released in 1990. He was voted in as the first black president of South Africa in 1994 and served for five years, after which he declined to run for a further term, preferring instead to retire and concentrate on combating HIV/AIDS and poverty through the Nelson Mandela Foundation. During his lifetime he received more than 250 honours, including the Nobel Peace Prize in 1993, and Nelson Mandela Day is now celebrated internationally each year (see p. 27).

Here's a short synopsis of his very long life and history:

- 1918: Born on 18 July
- 1942: Joins the African National Congress (ANC)
- 1944: Marries his first wife, Evelyn, but they were divorced in 1958
- 1958: Marries Winnie Mandela on 14 June
- 1964: Sentenced to life imprisonment after he is found guilty of committing sabotage against South Africa's government
- 1990: Released from prison on 11 February

- 1994: Becomes South Africa's first black President
- 1996: Visits Brixton
- 1998: Marries his third wife, Graça Machel, in 1998
- 2013: His autobiography *A Long Road to Freedom* released that April
- 2013: Dies in December
- 2014: Film *A Long Walk to Freedom* released

Sustained international and UK-based action and events contributed to bringing the apartheid regime to worldwide attention. This included:

- Protest against the all-white South Africa rugby and cricket teams touring the UK.
- A four-year picket during the 1980s outside the South African Embassy, Trafalgar Square.
- Boycotting the sale of South African goods.
- In 1984 the protest song 'Free Nelson Mandela' was released by the British two-tone band the Specials.
- In 1988 Sting, Whitney Houston, Stevie Wonder and Miriam Makeba headlined Nelson Mandela's 70th birthday tribute at Wembley Stadium.

Mandela Street in Camden is one of many streets named after Nelson Mandela. Other streets include: Nelson Mandela Road, Greenwich; Mandela Close in Stonebridge Park, Brent; Mandela Way, Bermondsey; Nelson Mandela Close, Muswell Hill.

The bronze statue of Nelson Mandela shown here – fashioned by Ian Walters, who died in 2006 – was unveiled on 29 August 2007 in Parliament Square. In attendance was Gordon Brown, the then UK prime minister, Mandela himself and his wife Graça Machel. The statue – which is just 9 foot (2.7 m) high – stands on an unusually low plinth, apparently reflecting Mandela's personal wish, so that he could be closer to the people and they could interact with the statue. Mandela's outwards arms symbolise an embracing and united South Africa as he welcomes the rest of the world.

A bust of Nelson Mandela – again created by English sculptor Ian Walters, who was a staunch supporter of the anti-apartheid movement – is situated outside on the first-floor level of the Royal Festival Hall. Originally commissioned by Ken Livingstone when he was leader of the Greater London Council (GLC), it was erected in 1985 and unveiled by fellow South African freedom fighter Oliver Tambo. However, the original fibreglass statue was vandalised repeatedly and set on fire. Eventually, the new bust was set on a high plinth and recast in bronze.

JIMI HENDRIX
SINGER AND GUITARIST (1942-70)
23 Brook Street, Mayfair, W1K 4HA

Jimi Hendrix was born Johnny Allen Hendrix in 1942 in America, but in 1946 he changed his name change to James Marshall Hendrix in honour of his late brother. At the age of 15, he began playing the guitar, subsequently – following a year serving with the army – playing the circuit from 1962 onwards in an attempt to gain experience. He joined the Isley Brothers backing band for a short while, then joined Little Richard's band, with whom he stayed until 1965.

In 1966 Hendrix moved to England and within months had three hits in the UK charts. He achieved world fame, became the world's highest-paid performer and headlined at various music festivals, including Monterey (1967), Woodstock (1969) and the Isle of Wight (1970). Seen as a pioneer among his peers, he was awarded many accolades for his work in the music industry, but on 18 September 1970, Hendrix, aged 27, was found unconscious after a drug overdose. An ambulance was called, but he was pronounced dead by the time he arrived at St Mary Abbott's Hospital in Kensington. He was buried in Washington, USA.

The English Heritage plaque shown here can be found in Brook Street, and was unveiled in 1997 by Pete Townshend. A statue of Jimi, erected in 2006, stands in the grounds of Dimbola Lodge on the Isle of Wight. Numerous commemorative plaques can be found across the UK in various venues and clubs.

STUART HALL

ACADEMIC, WRITER AND CULTURAL STUDIES PIONEER (1932–2014)
Institute of Visual Arts,
16 John Islip Street, SW1P 4JU

A persistent challenger of British hegemony from its colonial legacy, in 1991 Stuart Hall presented the BBC 2 series *Redemption Song* that explored the history and culture of the Caribbean. From 1997 to 2000 he served on the Runnymede Commission on the Future of Multi-Ethnic Britain. He was also involved with the Black Arts Movement (BAM) and was the founding chair of Iniva (the Institute of International Visual Arts) and Autograph (the Association of Black Photographers). The artist John Akomfrah's documentary *The Stuart Hall Project* (2013) tells his story from his roots in colonial Jamaica to his assertion of a black British identity, set to the soundtrack of black American jazz trumpeter Miles Davis, who Hall admired.

The Stuart Hall Library acts as a critical and creative hub for Iniva, which was founded in 1994. The library reopened at its new site in Pimlico (on the Chelsea College of Arts campus) in 2019. Iniva evolved from the 1980s BAM to provide recognition of and space for black art and artists. Its specialist reference-only collection focuses on art by people of African, Caribbean, Asian and Latin American descent. The library is open to all and membership is free. It also hosts regular talks, tours and events on issues surrounding the politics of race, class and gender.

MODERN MARTYRS
SCULPTURES (1998)
Westminster Abbey, 20 Deans Yard, SW1P 3PA

16

The spaces above the west gate on Westminster Abbey had been empty since the Middle Ages. Then, in 1998, the Modern Martyrs statues were unveiled by the Queen and the Duke of Edinburgh.

The martyrs represent religious persecution and oppression in each continent. A team of four sculptors led by Tim Crawley carved the figures. Each statue has a story about how they came to be there. However, most people fail to see the black representative statues.

– The second statue from the left commemorates Manche Masemola, a young South African girl who was murdered by her mother after she refused to stop visiting the missionaries who came to her town to convert them to Christianity.

- The third statue is that of priest, Janani Luwum, who was assassinated during the reign of Idi Amin, Uganda's ruthless president in the 1970s.
- In the centre stands Dr Martin Luther King Jr, the famous African American Baptist minister and civil rights leader who was assassinated in 1968.
- The ninth statue is that of Lucian Tapiedi, a Papua New Guinea priest who was murdered by the Japanese during the Second World War.

The full list of statues is as follows:

1. St Maximilian Kolbe
2. Manche Masemola
3. Janani Luwum
4. Grand Duchess Elizabeth
5. Martin Luther King Jr
6. St Oscar Romero
7. Dietrich Bonhoeffer
8. Esther John
9. Lucian Tapiedi
10. Wang Zhiming

MEMORIAL GATES
MONUMENT (2002)
Constitution Hill, Green Park, SW1A 1AA

The Memorial Gates were unveiled in November 2002 by the Queen. Designed by Liam O'Connor and built by Geoffrey Osborne Ltd, they commemorate the five million Commonwealth volunteers who took part in the First and Second World Wars from the Caribbean, Africa and the Indian subcontinent. The structure is made up of four Portland stone balustrades and cast bronze, along with bronze urns that sit atop the balustrades. The gates are situated at the upper end of Constitution Hill near to Hyde Park. Plans for the memorial were prepared by the Memorial Gates Trust.

Ben Okri OBE, poet, Booker Prize-winning author and one of Africa's leading writers, was asked to provide the inscription on the memorial. He chose to use the words 'Our Future Is Greater Than Our Past', which is the final line of his poem 'Turn On Your Light'.

THE JAMAICA WINE HOUSE
COFFEE HOUSE (1652)
St Michael's Alley, Cornhill, EC3V 9DS

This coffee house, although not the first in the UK, was opened in 1652 by Pasqua Rosée, an Armenian born in the early seventeenth century. He was manservant to Daniel Edwards, a trader, who helped him set up the establishment. The building stands in St Michael's Alley in the City of London with a sign that reads: 'Here Stood the first London Coffee House at the sign of Pasqua Rosee's Head 1652.'

Coffee growing started in the hills of Ethiopia and somehow over the years found its way to Turkey, where many people mistakenly think it originated.

The word 'coffee' came into the English language around 1598, originating from the Arabic '*qahhwat al-bun*', meaning 'wine of the bean'.

There were over a thousand coffee houses in London, but a select few focused on the needs of the London merchants trading at the nearby Royal Exchange and Lloyds. The coffee houses of London were frequented by merchants and sea captains who traded around the world, particularly in Africa, America, the Caribbean, India and China. As well as providing lodgings and food, and serving as postal collection spots and the focal point for getting the latest news from far-flung places, they would have been places where the business of slave trading occurred.

This site was also frequented by celebrities of the time such as Dickens, Pepys and Christopher Wren. Destroyed during the Great Fire of London, the building was quickly rebuilt with support from the wealthy merchants who frequented it. The current building is the third on the site, and today the Jamaica Coffee House is known by two different names: the Jamaica Wine House and Todd's Wine Bar. It is now part of the Shepherd Neame chain of pubs and is managed by one of the few black female pub managers in London, Lee Anderson.

FRANCES BARBER
SERVANT AND FREEMAN (c.1742–1801)

Dr Samuel Johnson's House, 17 Gough Square, Holborn, EC3A 3DE

Frances Barber was born into slavery in Jamaica and brought to London around 1750 by Colonel Richard Bathurst after he sold his plantation. The young Barber was entrusted into the care of Samuel Johnson, author, lexicographer and compiler of the first comprehensive English dictionary. Johnson believed in the expansion of Christianity worldwide, and he was opposed to slavery. Barber was a tutee within the household and also worked as a servant.

Bathurst died in 1755 and granted Barber his freedom in his will. In 1776 Barber married a white British woman and had children and later grandchildren. When Johnson died in 1784, he left Barber a sizeable inheritance and worldly effects. Barber relocated his family to Johnson's hometown of Lichfield, Staffordshire, and opened a school. Although the school proved short lived, Barber and his descendants settled in the area, dying and being buried there in 1801.

This BBC History Project plaque at Dr Samuel Johnson's house was unveiled in 2016. Attendees at the event included Barber's descendants.

PHILLIS WHEATLEY
POET (c.1753–84)

9 Aldgate High Street, EC3N 1AH

Phillis Wheatley is said to have been born in West Africa and kidnapped aged around eight. Although she survived the 'Middle Passage' (crossing the Atlantic), by the time she arrived in Boston, America, she was deemed too weak to work on the plantation. She was sold to the Wheatley family, who put her to work as a servant. However, it wasn't long before her aptitude for language was recognised and she was soon being taught how to read, write and spell, as well as Latin and Greek. She was brought to England to meet Archibald Bell, who first published Wheatley's 1773 book of poetry titled *Poems on Various Subjects, Religious and Moral*. While in London, Wheatley visited Greenwich and the British Museum, and had an audience with the Mayor of London. She was released from slavery by her owners soon after they died, but was left in poverty, and although she married shortly afterwards, her life spiralled into tragedy. In 1784 Wheatley's husband was thrown into a debtor's prison and she was unable to care for their sickly child or herself. She died aged just 31, followed by the death of her child.

This Nubian Jak plaque was unveiled in July 2019 in Aldgate on the side of the Dorsett City Hotel. The building is said to be the original site of her publisher's. The opening event was attended by a representative of the US Embassy and students from Canon High School, who performed poetry dedicated to Wheatley.

JONATHAN STRONG & GRANVILLE SHARP
ENSLAVED YOUTH AND ABOLITIONIST (1765)
St Bartholomew's Hospital, West Smithfield, EC1A 7BE

A Jamaican planter named David Lisle brought one of his slaves, Jonathan Strong, to London. In 1765 he beat Strong with a pistol, leaving him nearly blind, and threw him out. Brothers William and Granville Sharp, a surgeon and a clerk at the Ordnance Office, rescued him, and arranged and paid for four months of medical treatment at St Bartholomew's hospital. On his discharge they also found him work.

Two years later, Lisle spotted Strong and paid two slave-catchers to have him thrown into prison to await shipment back to Jamaica, upon which Lisle would receive payment for his 'property'. Strong was able to get a message to Granville, who, despite having no legal training, took up the challenge and successfully argued his case at court. Granville went on to assist other runaway slaves and fought for a definitive judgement on the legality of slavery in the UK. In 1772 the landmark case of James Somerset, a slave sold in Virginia and baptised in London, was brought before Lord Chief Justice Mansfield. Aware of the financial implications, his carefully worded judgement ruled that slave owners could not legally remove slaves once in England. Strong died in 1773 and Sharp in 1813. The slave trade was abolished in 1807, and full freedom in the colonies came in 1838, but control of the lands and people continued.

A BBC History Project plaque was unveiled at St Bartholomew's Hospital, London, in September 2016. Attendees included hospital staff, lawyers and Granville Sharp's descendants.

GILT OF CAIN
MONUMENT (2008)
Fen Court Garden, Fen Court, Langbourn, EC3M 5BN

This structure, the *Gilt of Cain*, commemorates the abolition of Britain's transatlantic slave trade in 1807, which began the process of the emancipation of slaves throughout its Empire. The structure – in the former churchyard of St Mary Woolnoth, which used to stand there – was unveiled by Desmond Tutu in 2008 and is situated in an area of the City of London with a strong historical connection to the abolitionist movement of the eighteenth and nineteenth centuries.

Devised by Michael Visocchi, the sculpture has three steps that lead to what could be seen as an ecclesiastical pulpit, but that could also represent a slave auctioneer's podium. The columns evoke stems of sugar cane and are positioned to suggest an anonymous crowd, a group of slaves or a congregation gathered to listen to a speaker. The structure also features a poem of the same name by Lemn Sissay, poet, author and broadcaster. The words are etched on the pulpit and columns, and use the coded language of the City's stock exchange intermingled with terms associated with the slave trade. Sissay was the official poet for the London 2012 Olympics.

MUSEUM OF LONDON
BLACK HISTORY EXHIBITIONS
150 London Wall, EC2Y 5HN

Located close to the Barbican Centre, the Museum of London holds the largest urban history collection in the world. With over six million objects, the museum represents black Londoners through their permanent and temporary exhibitions throughout the year. It will relocate to Smithfield Market in 2022.

CASH
BUT SPIRIT
YOU ASK,
BROTHERS
I ANSWER
BY SPIRIT BY
MY NAME,

NETWORK
SCULPTURE (2014)
1 Old Street Yard, EC1Y 8AF

24

This contemporary statue was created by sculptor Thomas J. Price. The male is called *Network* and was unveiled in 2014. Its current home is at the White Collar Factory, East London.

In 2020 Price released the female version of the same statue called *Reaching Out*. It can be found at Three Mills Green, E3 3DU. Both bronze figures are 2.7 m (9 ft) high and depict the users on their mobiles. The artist creates his works using the lost-wax process, also called cire-perdue, a method of metal casting first used thousands of years ago in Africa, as with the Benin Bronzes in the thirteenth century. The artist pours metal into a mould that has been made using a wax model.

Price was born in 1981 to a British mother and Jamaican father. He studied at the Royal College of Art and lives and works in Deptford, south London. His work is engaged with issues of representation and perception in society and art. It also raises questions and invites conversations regarding who we put on pedestals, and why. His figures represent everyday black people who are unheroic and are getting on with daily life.

Price, alongside fellow artist Veronica Ryan, has been commissioned by Hackney Council to create two new individual public artworks celebrating Hackney's Windrush generation. They will be the first permanent public sculptures in the UK to do so and will be unveiled in 2021.

AUTOGRAPH
GALLERY
Rivington Place, Shoreditch, EC2A 3BA

Autograph, the Association of Black Photographers, has been based at Rivington Place, Shoreditch, since 2007. The five-storey building and art gallery space was designed by award-winning architect Sir David Adjaye, who went on to create the National Museum of African American History and Culture in Washington, DC, which opened in 2016.

Autograph was founded in 1988 to support black photographers and originally operated in Brixton as an agency initiating art projects. Professor Stuart Hall acted as chair for Autograph and Iniva (the Institute of International Visual Arts). As an arts charity, Autograph is dedicated to the development and public presentation of culturally diverse visual arts. Its selected works highlight issues of identity, representation, human rights and social justice through photography and film. The gallery holds free exhibitions and hosts a programme of talks, educational activities and collaborations with a wide range of community groups. Autograph also works internationally promoting exhibitions, events and publications concerned with photography.

ERIC & JESSICA HUNTLEY
COMMUNITY ACTIVISTS AND EDUCATORS (b.1929 & 1927-2013)
Huntley Archives, London Metropolitan Archives,
40 Northampton Road, Farringdon, EC1R 0HB

The Huntleys founded Bogle L'Ouverture Publications in 1968, the name honouring two Caribbean leaders: Paul Bogle of Jamaica and Toussaint L'Ouverture of Haiti. The Huntleys' bookshop-cum-meeting-hub, New Beacon Books, was later renamed after Guyanese writer and activist Dr Walter Rodney following his assassination in 1980. The couple initiated and campaigned in a number of movements, including the British Black Panthers, Black Supplementary Schools in the 1970s and the Black People's Day of Action march in 1981. In 2005 they deposited their archives at the London Metropolitan Archives (LMA) in Islington, north London, where they can still be accessed, and since 2006 the Annual Huntley Conference (see p. 26) is held there in February to continue promoting the educational and cultural legacy of

Black British history. Jessica died in 2013.

A Nubian Jak plaque was unveiled in October 2018 at Coldershaw Road, Ealing (see p. 98), to recognise the work of Eric and Jessica Huntley. The bronze bust of Jessica, shown here, was created by the artist George 'Fowakan' Kelly and, like the archives, resides at the LMA. Eric and Jessica were both born in 1920s British Guiana (now Guyana) and came to London in the 1950s.

THE BLACKFRIAR
RELIEF STATUE (1958)
Corner of Pocock Street and Blackfriars Street, SE1 0BT

27

This relief was unveiled in 1958 and is a stylised representation of a Blackfriar with African facial features riding on a donkey. It can be viewed very high up on the side of a building in Pocock Street, Blackfriars, above the shops.

The stone relief is in the shape of a cross and it may be that it depicts one of the Dominican monks who took orders in Blackfriars Priory during the thirteenth century.

The relief was sculpted by Edward Bainbridge Copnall (1903–73), who was born in South Africa but brought up in England. He was also president of the Royal Society of Sculptors in the 1960s.

THE AFRICA CENTRE
CONFERENCE CENTRE (1964)
66 Great Suffolk Street, SE1 0BL

The Africa Centre first opened in 1964 and provided a cultural and political hub for the African diasporas in London. Based in Covent Garden, the centre held art exhibitions, dances, conferences and cultural events as well as housing meeting rooms, a bar and bookshop.

In 2013 the Africa Centre moved to its new site at Great Suffolk Street, Southwark, and in 2014 it celebrated its Golden Jubilee. A giant steel 'Corten Head' sculpture by the Nigerian British artist Sokari Douglas Camp CBE graces the hub entrance at Union Yard Arches.

The organisation aims to build on its heritage by constructing a centre fit for the twenty-first century. The planned transformation of the building will include: a café, kitchen, event-spaces, bar, gallery, learning and research centre, meeting rooms and broadcast suite. The centre's mission rests upon five pillars: Culture; Entrepreneurship & Innovation; Community; Education; and Intellectual Leadership. The Young Africa Centre (YAC) will provide a platform for the voices of young people of African descent.

WAYNE MARQUES
BRITISH TRANSPORT POLICE OFFICER (1979)
Southwark Cathedral, London Bridge, SE1 9DA

In the exterior corner of Humphrey's Yard on the north side of Southwark Cathedral three new corbels (elaborate stone carved brackets) were installed in 2018. Positioned high up, the trio join a row of (unknown) faces that date back to the 1820s. The new additions replaced some badly deteriorated ones and depict Evelyn Sharp, a local suffragist, and Doorkins the cathedral cat (2008–20). The male face in the centre is PC Wayne Marques, a British Transport Police Officer, who was one of the first responders to the London Bridge terrorist attack in June 2017.

The commissioned works were created by student carvers at the City & Guilds College in Kennington, in collaboration with children at Southwark's Cathedral School, who drew from the local history of the community. (A fourth new corbel representing Borough Market and

depicting its produce can be seen on the south side of the building.) PC
Marques was present with his family at the installation of the corbels.
The sculpture depicts the head scars he received fighting off the knife-
wielding attackers armed only with his baton, and incorporates his
British Transport Police badge. Eight people were killed in the attack. In
2018 Marques received the George Medal for his heroic action.

MARY SEACOLE

NURSE AND AUTHOR (1805-81)

St Thomas's Hospital, SE1 7GA

Mary Seacole was born in Jamaica in 1805 to a Scottish soldier and a 'free' Creole woman. Her mother ran a boarding house, which doubled up as a convalescent home, and practised as a doctress using natural herbal medicines. Seacole followed in the same path. She worked in Jamaica and Panama, and her travels took her to London, Haiti and Cuba. When her offer to work as a volunteer nurse in the Crimea was rejected, she set off and established herself there independently, becoming known as 'Mother Seacole' among the troops. Shortly after the war, having returned to England, Seacole was declared bankrupt, but when the press highlighted her predicament, a series of fund-raising initiatives rescued her from poverty. Her bestselling autobiography *Wonderful Adventures of Mrs Seacole in Many Lands* in 1857 is still in print to this day. Seacole died in Paddington, London, and is buried in St Mary's Catholic Cemetery, Kensal Green.

Established in 2004, the Mary Seacole Memorial Statue Appeal (MSA) campaigned to provide a lasting legacy for her work. Designed by sculptor Martin Jennings, this full-sized bronze statue stands in the gardens of St Thomas' Hospital and was unveiled by Baroness Floella Benjamin in 2016. It is the UK's first named statue of a black woman. The figure marches forward on a raised, inscribed slate. The five-ton textured disc behind her reproduces an impression of the actual ground in the Crimea. In 2004 a BBC survey voted Seacole 'the Greatest Black Briton'. Seacole has numerous commemorations, which include an oil portrait by Albert Challen dating from 1869 and exhibited at the National Portrait Gallery (see p. 39), a bust sculpted in 1871 by Count Gleichen (Queen Victoria's nephew) and an English Heritage plaque at 14 Soho Square, Westminster. In 2012 Southbank Mosaics created ten portraits of significant Lambeth women, all of which are on display on the exterior wall at Morley College, King Edward Walk. Artist Alejandra Casimiro Herrera produced the tiled image of Seacole.

The MSA campaign transitioned into the Mary Seacole Trust in 2016 and continues to build on Seacole's legacy to promote fairness and equality through its education and diversity leadership programmes.

THE BRITISH LIBRARY
INSTALLATION (2019)
Tate Modern, Bankside, SE1 9TG

In 2019 a new permanent exhibition titled *The British Library* opened at the Tate Modern in London. The work, created by Yinka Shonibare, celebrates the diversity of Britons and Britain. *The British Library* features 6,328 books covered in Shonibare's trademark Dutch wax fabric. Emblazoned in gold leaf on the spine of 2,700 of these books is the name of first- or second-generation immigrants who have made significant contributions to British culture and history. The installation also includes a website with an A–Z index.

Among the names are Adrian Lester, Ainsley Harriott, Alex Wheatle, Beverley Knight, Benjamin Zephaniah, Bernie Grant, Chris Ofili, C. L. R. James, Claudia Jones, Cy Grant, Darcus Howe, David Adjaye, David

Lammy, Doreen Lawrence, Dotun Adebayo, Floella Benjamin, Frank Bowling, Frank Crichlow, Gary Younge, Idris Elba, John Archer, John Akomfrah, Johnson Beharry, Khadambi Asalache, Laura Mvula, Lemn Sissay, Levi Roots, Marcus Garvey, Marianne Jean-Baptiste, Pauline Black, Rageh Omaar, Rio Ferdinand, Rudolph Walker, Rudy Narayan, Sam Selvon, Samuel Coleridge-Taylor, Sonia Boyce, Steve McQueen, Stuart Hall, Walter Tull, Winifred Atwell and Zadie Smith. Others include those who have opposed immigration, such as Enoch Powell and Nigel Farage. Some books have been left without names, indicating that Britain's history is still to be written and is ongoing.

The British Library was first shown in Brighton in 2014. It also featured at the Turner Contemporary in Margate, in 2016, and in the Diaspora Pavilion of the 2017 Venice Biennale. Shonibare also created *Nelson's Ship in a Bottle* (2010) (see p. 170).

JAMAICA ROAD
STREET
Bermondsey, SE1

This road has close links to the slave trade. Many of those who were taken from Africa were settled in Jamaica, and slave ships returning from the Caribbean would dock at the nearby West India Docks on the Thames. The prosperity brought by the trade was reflected in the name of a fine building that once stood in the area, visited by Samuel Pepys in 1664 – Jamaica House – which the street was subsequently named after in the 1860s.

ROBERT WEDDERBURN
RADICAL LEADER AND ANTI-SLAVERY ADVOCATE (1762-1835)
337 Kennington Park Road, Oval, SE11 4PW

St Mark's Church at Kennington Park Road, Oval, was built in 1824. It forms one of the four 'Waterloo' churches built following Napoleon's defeat and named after the four Gospels (Matthew, Mark, Luke and John). On the Kennington Park side of the church, mounted panels record the local history. On the second panel, relating to 1789, it states: 'one of the first "black" preachers, the radical Robert Wedderburn born to a West African slave woman in Jamaica, spoke on this site'.

Robert was the illegitimate son of plantation owner James Wedderburn. His father sold his mother Rosanna while she was pregnant with him. Although he was born free, he endured the atrocities of plantation life. Robert later ran away to join the navy and came to England in 1778, aged 16.

He was drawn to the black community in St Giles and became involved in radical politics, opening his own Unitarian chapel in Soho as a meeting place, where he gave sermons. Wedderburn called for a revolution of the poor in Europe and the slaves in the Caribbean. He spoke out and circulated pamphlets against Christianity and the clergy. In 1820 he was sentenced to two years' imprisonment for blasphemy.

In 1824, he published *The Horrors of Slavery*, which was widely circulated by the abolitionist cause. He continued campaigning for freedom of speech and was later imprisoned again. His exact date of death is unknown.

MAYA ANGELOU

POET, WRITER AND CIVIL RIGHTS ACTIVIST (1928–2014)
Kennington Park, SE11 5TY

The standing stone civilian memorial to the Second World War victims at Kennington Park was unveiled in October 2006 – the fruition of a fund-raising project initiated by the Friends of Kennington Park. Created by sculptor Richard Kindersley, the engraved stone bears a dedication around the edges to wartime suffering and to the 50 men, women and children killed during the Blitz when a 50-pound bomb destroyed an air-raid shelter near the spot in 1940.

The central inscription from African American poet, writer and civil rights activist Maya Angelou (1928–2014) reads: 'History, despite its wrenching pain, cannot be unlived but if faced with courage need not be lived again.' Angelou recited the full poem, 'On the Pulse of Morning', at Bill Clinton's inauguration in 1993. In 2011 President Barack Obama quoted these same lines again to Angelou when he awarded her the Presidential Medal of Freedom. Angelou was the first black female to deliver the Presidential Inaugural poem and in 2021 Amanda Gorman followed in the footsteps of her role model at President Joe Biden's inauguration, with her poem, 'The Hill We Climb'. Gorman also wore a birdcage ring gifted to her by Oprah Winfrey in honour of Angelou, whose works included her autobiography, *I Know Why the Caged Bird Sings*, and a collection of poetry that includes the seminal 'Still I Rise'.

Angelou visited London on a number of occasions and performed at the Lewisham Theatre (now the Broadway Theatre) in Catford, where she was a patron. She died aged 86 in 2014.

BENIN BRONZES

PLAQUES (SIXTEENTH–SEVENTEENTH CENTURY)
British Museum, Great Russell Street, Bloomsbury, WC1B 3DG

A selection of Benin bronzes can be viewed in the Africa Gallery at the British Museum, Bloomsbury. These 'bronzes' are made from a mixture of brass, wood, ceramic, ivory and other materials. They are examples of metal-working skill using the lost-wax casting process. Over a thousand bronzes would have decorated the wooden beams supporting the roof of the royal palace of the Kingdom of Benin.

Sections of the intricate sculptures date to the thirteenth century and were crafted by the Edo people in what is now modern-day Nigeria.

The bronzes glorified the Oba, the divine king, and depict court life, from noble dignitaries wearing ceremonial dress to naked royal servants. They also include depictions of long-haired hook-nosed European adventurers and traders. In 1897 Benin was seized by British forces and the bronzes were looted during a punitive expedition. The British Museum acquired two hundred pieces in 1898. Bronzes also went to other European museums and global collections. In 2016 George the Poet performed his 'Benin bronzes' poem at the British Museum as part of the Huge History Lesson.

THE PETRIE MUSEUM OF EGYPTIAN ARCHAEOLOGY
MUSEUM
University College London, Malet Place, WC1E 6BT

This museum was founded and named after Flinders Petrie, the archaeologist who went to Egypt in the nineteenth century to excavate dozens of major sites. The museum is part of the University College of London (UCL) and ranks as one of the world's leading collections of Egyptian and Sudanese material. It holds over 80,000 objects, including the Tarkhan Dress, from Egypt, reckoned to be the earliest garment so far discovered; ancient wills written on papyrus; and a collection of some of the oldest afro combs ever found.

MARY PRINCE
AUTHOR (1788-1833)
Senate House, Malet Street, Bloomsbury, WC1E 7HU

Mary Prince was born into slavery in Bermuda in 1788. Sold several times before she was brought by new owners to London, she managed to escape from the family she worked for, fleeing to a Moravian church where she met Thomas Pringle, an abolitionist, who listened to her story. He introduced her to Susanna Strickland, who wrote down her story. Prince's autobiography was published in 1831 as the *History of Mary Prince A West Indian Slave, Related by Herself.* The book was a roaring success and sold out. After publication, there were two cases of libel brought against Thomas Pringle, and Mary twice had to defend the work in court. He won the first case and lost the second. Mary herself was sued for libel by her previous owner due to the things she said about him in the book. Supported by the abolitionist movement, she won the case. Pringle also sued a newspaper for defamation of his character. After 1833, Mary disappears from history. Whether she returned as a free woman to Bermuda – which by the following year had abolished slavery – is not known.

A Nubian Jak bronze plaque was unveiled in November 2007 at Senate House in Bloomsbury where Mary Prince used to live. Attendees included MP Diane Abbott and the Mayor of Camden.

YMCA CLUB

HOME OF BRITAIN'S FIRST CIVIL RIGHTS MOVEMENT
111 Great Russell Street, WC1B 3NP

In 2019 the Nubian Jak Community Trust commemorated Harold Moody's work in establishing 'The League of Coloured Peoples' in 1931 with a plaque at the Central YMCA. Moody (see p. 136), a committed Christian, first sought help in finding accommodation here when he came to London in 1904.

AFRICAN NATIONAL CONGRESS

POLITICAL PARTY
28 Penton Street, N1 9PW

The African National Congress (ANC) headquarters was based at this address from 1978 to 1994, the latter being the year in which Nelson Mandela became President. It was used for coordinating anti-apartheid activity in the UK and to bring attention to the atrocities being legitimised under the white South Africa government.

In 1982 the building was bombed as part of a likely assassination attempt on ANC President Oliver Tambo's life. Windows up to 400 yards away shattered and several buildings were damaged. Fortunately, no one was seriously hurt. After the Truth and Reconciliation Commission was set up in South Africa by Nelson Mandela, the culprits were revealed to be South African police officers. The ANC moved out of the building in 1994 and it was taken over by an African charity

that remained there until 2006. This Nubian Jak plaque was unveiled in 2017 by His Excellency Dr Zola Skweyiya, High Commissioner for South Africa; Councillor Terry Stacy JP, leader of Islington Council; and Jak Beula, chair of the Nubian Jak Community Trust.

SIDNEY BECHET
MUSICIAN (1897-1959)

27 Conway Street, Camden, W1T 6BB

Sidney Joseph Bechet was born in New Orleans in 1897 to a middle-class family. Learning to play several musical instruments that were kept around the house, mostly by teaching himself, he decided finally to specialise in the clarinet. At the age of six, he started playing with his brother's band at a family birthday party. Then, as a young man, in the spring of 1919, he travelled to New York City, where he joined Will Marion Cook's Syncopated Orchestra. Soon afterwards, the orchestra travelled to Europe; almost immediately upon arriving in the UK, they performed at the Royal Philharmonic Hall in London. They were warmly received, Bechet proving especially popular. It was while he was in London that he discovered the straight soprano saxophone, an instrument that he made his own. On 15 September 1925, Bechet and other members of the Revue Nègre, including Josephine Baker, sailed for the Continent, arriving at Cherbourg, France, on 22 September.

In Paris, according to his autobiography, he accidentally shot a woman while trying to shoot a musician who had insulted him, a crime for which he was imprisoned in Paris for 11 months. After his release, he was deported to New York, arriving soon after the stock market crash there of 1929. He joined Noble Sissle's orchestra, which toured in Germany and Russia; then he moved permanently to France in 1950 following a surge in his popularity there after his performance as a soloist at the Paris Jazz Fair. In 1951 he married Elisabeth Ziegler in Antibes, and three years later the poet Philip Larkin wrote a poem about him called 'For Sidney Bechet'. Shortly before his death, Bechet dictated his autobiography, *Treat It Gentle*, to Al Rose, a record producer and radio host. Bechet died in Garches, near Paris, of lung cancer on 14 May 1959 on his 62nd birthday. He is buried in a local cemetery.

A Nubian Jak plaque was erected in November 2014 and unveiled by Bechet's son Daniel. The street in which it hangs was called Southampton Street when Bechet lived there, this subsequently being renamed after the Second World War. The plaque is unusual in that it was raised by public subscription.

FURTHER AFIELD

MUSEUM OF LONDON DOCKLANDS
EXHIBITION
No. 1 Warehouse, West India Quay, E14 4AL

Originally a warehouse for the sugar that came from the Caribbean, the Museum of London Docklands houses the permanent exhibition: 'London, Sugar & Slavery: 1600 – today'. This includes a display of the names of the slave ships that set sail from London and a copy of the book, *Letters of the Late Ignatius Sancho, who was born on a slave ship*. The museum, though, does more than simply illustrate how the slave trade shaped London. The 'Windrush Stories' exhibition is a collection of oral histories, articles and photographs from some of the Windrush generation, including Sam King, who arrived on the *HMT Empire Windrush* at Tilbury Dock and went on to become the first black Mayor of Southwark (see p. 140).

7 EDGEWARE ROAD
GOODGE STREET
GLOUCESTER PLACE
BAKER STREET
MARYLEBONE ROAD
GREAT PORTLAND STREET
MARYLEBONE FLYOVER
PRAED STREET
SUSSEX GARDENS
EDGWARE ROAD
GLOUCESTER PLACE
SEYMOUR ST
OXFORD STREET
OXFORD CIRCUS
REGENT STREET
NEW BOND STREET
LANCASTER GATE
BAYSWATER ROAD
CUMBERLAND GATE

6 HYDE PARK
PARK LANE
GREEN PARK
A4
GREEN PARK
PICCADILLY
ST JAMES'S PARK

HYDE PARK CORNER

5 KNIGHTSBRIDGE
BROMPTON ROAD
GROSVENOR PLACE

11 SLOANE STREET

4 SOUTH KENSINGTON
EATON SQUARE
SLOANE SQUARE
BUCKINGHAM PALACE ROAD
VAUXHALL BRIDGE ROAD
ROCHESTER ROW
BELGRAVE ROAD

FULHAM ROAD
SYDNEY STREET
PIMLICO ROAD
PIMLICO

16 ROYAL HOSPITAL ROAD
OAKLEY STREET
KING'S ROAD
CHELSEA EMBANKMENT
QUEENSTOWN ROAD
GROSVENOR ROAD

CHEYNE WALK
RIVER THAMES
ALBERT BRIDGE ROAD
BATTERSEA BRIDGE ROAD

BATTERSEA PARK
BATTERSEA PARK

IMPERIAL WHARF

18 BATTERSEA PARK ROAD
LATCHMERE ROAD
QUEENSTOWN ROAD
SILVERTHORNE ROAD
19 WANDSWORTH ROAD

1	WILLIAM AND ELLEN CRAFT	**8**	DR JOHN ALCINDOR	**15**	KELSO COCHRANE
2	CETSHWAYO KAMPANDE	**9**	AMY ASHWOOD GARVEY	**16**	BOB MARLEY
3	CONNIE MARK	**10**	LEARIE CONSTANTINE	**17**	BOB MARLEY & THE WAILERS
4	FREDERICK DOUGLASS	**11**	ELISABETH WELCH	**18**	JOHN ARCHER
5	MEMORIAL TO THE GREAT EXHIBITION	**12**	CLAUDIA JONES	**19**	KHADAMBI ASALACHE
6	ALBERT MEMORIAL AFRICA	**13**	NOTTING HILL CARNIVAL		
7	HENRY SYLVESTER WILLIAMS	**14**	ARTHUR STANLEY WINT		

2

WEST LONDON

When in the 1950s white racist gangs began to persecute black people in the Notting Hill area, those living there put out a call to other black people to come to their aid. People from as far afield as Brixton responded in a bid to help fight the racists, putting together Molotov cocktails to throw at the racists who attacked them, and sometimes fighting in hand-to-hand combat. Years later, and partly in response to these racial tensions, the large black community, including many Trinidadians, would go on to create the Notting Hill Carnival.

Although having smaller black communities, areas such as Merton and Kingston have associations with some notable black people. Cesar Picton, for example, became a very rich man in Kingston, and Haile Selassie lived there for a short while, a bust of him having subsequently been erected in Cannizaro Park.

WILLIAM & ELLEN CRAFT

ANTI-SLAVERY CAMPAIGNERS (1824–1900 & 1826–1891)

Craft Court, 55–57 Glenthorne Road, Hammersmith, W6 0LJ

Both William and Ellen Craft were born into slavery in the southern state of Georgia, USA. They married in 1846 in a slave ceremony that was not recognised as legal. Nor could they live together, as they belonged to different masters, so they planned to escape to the northern states. The daughter of a white slave owner and mixed-raced mother, Ellen, resembling a white person, was able to pass as a male plantation owner, with William posing as her slave. Given that she could not read or write, she took the precaution of bandaging her arm to avoid having to sign any papers. (Teaching slaves to do so was a criminal offence in the southern states.)

The couple's escape in 1848 was successful, but, as fugitives, their future was uncertain, so they decided to sail to England. There they spent 19 years, first staying in Liverpool, then settling in Hammersmith, where they raised a family. The two of them toured the country speaking against slavery and recounting their experiences. In 1860 they published a written account, *Running a Thousand Miles for Freedom*. Then, after the American Civil War and the abolition of slavery in the USA in 1865, the Crafts returned to Georgia in 1868 and set up a farm.

A plaque to William and Ellen Craft was erected at this address in 1995 by Shepherd's Bush Housing Association. The Crafts had lived nearby in Cambridge Road.

CETSHWAYO KAMPANDE

KING OF THE ZULUS (c.1826–84)

18 Melbury Road, W14 8LT

Cetshwayo kaMpande was the last king of the Zulus in Southern Africa. The half-nephew of the infamous Zulu king Shaka Zulu, he murdered virtually his entire family and became king when his father died in 1873. At first, he was on friendly terms with the British troops that occupied the Transvaal area, but it wasn't long before they provoked him into a war by requiring him to hand over more and more of his land, which he was reluctant to do.

In 1879 his refusal to do so led to the Battle of Isandlwana, won by the Zulus. However, the British got their own back at the Battle of Rorke's Drift and, finally, the Battle of Ulundi, after which Cetshwayo was exiled, first to Cape Town and then to London. While there he met with Queen Victoria to plead for the British to come out of Zululand, but to no avail. Eventually, when war broke out in Zululand between the various clans, the British tried to reinstall Cetshwayo as king, but by that time it was too late. He died in 1884 in South Africa, and several parts of that country are now named after him.

Cetshwayo kaMpande once stayed at this address, and an English Heritage plaque was unveiled here in 2006.

CONNIE MARK

COMMUNITY ACTIVIST (1923–2007)

Mary Seacole House, 24 Invermead Close, W6 0HQ

Constance Mark was born and raised in Jamaica. Her father taught in a British army school and she was privately educated under an English school system. During the Second World War she worked as a medical secretary for the Auxiliary Territorial Service at the British military hospital on the island and was later promoted to lance-corporal.

After the war, Mark moved to England with her first husband and worked as a secretary. Dedicating herself to charitable causes, she championed equality, education and the promotion of black history and culture. As well as founding the Friends of Mary Seacole, later renamed the Mary Seacole Memorial Association, in 1980, she was also instrumental in lobbying for the recognition and inclusion of West Indian servicemen and women in national war commemorations. In 1992 she received a British Empire Medal, followed by an OBE in 2001. She died aged 83 in 2007.

Initially erected in 2008, a Nubian Jak plaque has been reinstalled outside the Mary Seacole Housing Association (see Mary Seacole, p. 67). Attendees at its unveiling included Jamaica's High Commissioner, Jamaica Nurses UK, and publisher Margaret Busby OBE. The replacement coincided with what would have been Mark's 95th birthday.

FREDERICK DOUGLASS
SOCIAL REFORMER (1818-95)
Nell Gwynn House, Whiteheads Grove,
South Kensington, SW3 3AX

Born Frederick Augustus Washington Bailey, Douglass was the son of a slave woman and an unknown white man. His first 20 years were spent enslaved in Maryland, where he worked as a house servant, field hand and then shipyard labourer. Having learnt to read when he was young and sought to educate himself, he was determined to gain his freedom. Although he was imprisoned for one attempt to run away from his master, William Freeland, in 1835, he finally succeeded in 1838.

He settled in Massachusetts and married a free African American woman under his new name, Frederick Douglass. After giving a powerful speech at the Massachusetts Anti-Slavery Society he was enlisted as an agent for the abolitionist cause, going on later to become the leader of the movement. In 1845–6 he toured Britain and Ireland as well as publishing his autobiography, *Narrative of the Life of Frederick Douglass, an American Slave, Written by Himself.* While he was in London, British supporters helped him raise the money to purchase his freedom, and throughout the rest of his life Douglass continued to use his voice to improve the lives of African Americans. He died in Washington, DC.

A Nubian Jak plaque was unveiled at this address in 2013 in collaboration with the American Embassy. Douglass stayed here as the guest of British abolitionist George Thompson.

MEMORIAL TO THE GREAT EXHIBITION
MEMORIAL (1851)
Kensington Gore, South Kensington, SW7 2AP

The Great Exhibition (aka The Great Exhibition of the Works of Industry of All Nations) featured many new industrial developments from Britain and Europe that people had never seen before. Africa and the Caribbean colonies were represented in terms of the resources they brought to the British Empire. Over 6 million people attended the exhibition, which went on for six months from May to October 1851. It was opened by Queen Victoria and over

£30 million was raised, which helped to fund the building of a complex of Kensington museums including the Victoria and Albert Museum, and the Royal Albert Hall.

A collection of four bronze, granite and Portland stone statues was unveiled in 1851, and can be found at the back of the Royal Albert Hall. Sculpted by Joseph Durham (1814–77), they sit quietly at the back of the Hall, where most people simply pass them by. The work is one of four seated female figures around a central column, each one representing a different part of the world. The four females are Europe, America, Africa and Asia. This figure represents Africa. The black woman featured is unknown, though she may have been someone familiar to the artist. It was unusual for British sculptors to feature dreadlocks in their work.

ALBERT MEMORIAL – AFRICA
MEMORIAL (1872)
Albert Memorial, Kensington Gardens, W2 2UH

The Albert Memorial was commissioned by Queen Victoria in memory of her husband, Prince Albert, who died of typhoid in 1861. The cost of erecting the statue, £120K, was met by public subscription. Designed by Sir George Gilbert Scott, the memorial was opened in July 1872 by Queen Victoria herself. A statue of Albert was added three years later in 1875.

The figure shown here, created by William Theed Junior (1804–91), was unveiled in 1886. It is made of marble and is one of several on the Memorial. Named 'Africa', it comprises a set with Asia, America and Europe, each being situated on one of the outer corners. As well as people, the sculptures include an animal: a camel for Africa, a bison for the Americas, an elephant for Asia and a bull for Europe.

HENRY SYLVESTER WILLIAMS
PAN-AFRICAN ACTIVIST AND LAWYER (1869–1911)

38 Church Street, Marylebone, NW8 8EP

Henry Williams was born in Trinidad and started out as a teacher before moving to the USA to study Law. He later came to England, enrolled at King's College London and read for the bar at Gray's Inn in the 1890s, prior to the Law Society closing its door to black members in 1894.

In 1897 Williams founded the African Association as part of an anti-colonial movement with the primary aim of promoting and protecting the interests of all subjects of African descent. The 1884–5 Congress of Berlin had seen Britain and several European countries partitioning and exploiting Africa still further for its land, labour and resources. Williams, in tandem with the African Association, organised the first Pan-African Conference at London's Westminster Town Hall (now Caxton Hall) in 1900. Attendees at the three-day event came from Africa, the West Indies, the US and the UK. The Conference called for justice, equality and the right for self-government. Williams went on to set up branches of the Pan-African Conference in Jamaica, Trinidad and the USA. In 1906 he became the first black councillor in Marylebone, before he returned two years later to Trinidad, where he died in 1911. Pan-African Congress Conferences resumed in Paris in 1919 and then in London in 1921 and 1923.

The London Borough plaque that can be seen at this address was unveiled in 2007 by Henry Williams' grandson George Burns.

DR JOHN ALCINDOR
PHYSICIAN, PAN-AFRICANIST AND
FIRST WORLD WAR LOCAL HERO (1873–1924)

Harrow Road Health Centre, 209 Harrow Road, Paddington, W2 5EH

John Alcindor was born and grew up in Trinidad, where he studied at St Mary's College. He won a medical scholarship to study at Edinburgh University, from which he graduated in 1899, going on to work in London hospitals for several years before setting up his own practice. When the First World War broke out in 1914, he applied for but was refused a place in the Royal Army Medical Corps because of his 'colonial origin'. Instead, he signed up as a British Red Cross (BRC) volunteer and used his skills to help wounded soldiers returning from the battlefields. He was later awarded a BRC medal for his work.

A Pan-Africanist associated with Henry Sylvester Williams and his African Association (AA), Alcindor attended the first Pan-African Conference (PAC) in London – initiated by the AA – in 1900. He acted as the second president of the PAC in 1921 and spoke at the third in 1923. After the war, Alcindor settled in Paddington and served as Senior District Medical Officer of the borough from 1921 until his death in 1924. He was known locally as the 'black doctor of Paddington'.

In July 2014, a plaque to Alcindor was unveiled – with members of his family in attendance – on the site where he previously had his surgery. It is now a medical centre.

AMY ASHWOOD GARVEY
PAN-AFRICANIST AND HUMAN RIGHTS CAMPAIGNER (1897–1969)
1 Bassett Road, W10 6LA

Amy Ashwood was born in Jamaica into a middle-class family and met Marcus Garvey at a debating society in 1914. Together they founded the Universal Negro Improvement Association (UNIA), which was the most influential anti-colonial organisation in Jamaica up to 1938. Amy was UNIA's first secretary, a member of the management board and co-founder of the Ladies Auxiliary Wing.

In 1919 the couple married in New York where they set up the American headquarters of UNIA. However, the marriage was short-lived, and they divorced in 1922. Amy continued her political activism, travelling to London, the Caribbean and Africa to give lectures on black self-determination, Pan-Africanism and women's rights. She returned to London in 1934 and opened a jazz club, the Florence Mills Social Club, in Carnaby Street, Soho, which became a centre for Pan-Africanists.

In 1954 she opened the Afro Woman's Centre and Residential Club in Ladbroke Grove, going on to chair the official enquiry into race relations in London following the 1959 murder of Kelso Cochrane. She also worked with Claudia Jones to promote the event that would lay the foundations for the famous Notting Hill Carnival. In later life, with her health failing, Garvey returned to Jamaica, where she died in 1969.

In 2009 the Octavia Foundation, in partnership with the Nubian

Jak Community Trust, unveiled the plaque at 1 Bassett Road to Amy Ashwood Garvey. Attendees included the Jamaican High Commissioner and the Mayor of the Royal Borough of Kensington and Chelsea.

LEARIE CONSTANTINE
CRICKETER AND POLITICIAN (1901–71)
101 Lexham Gardens, Earl's Court, W8 6JG

Learie Constantine was born in Trinidad and first represented his country at cricket in 1921. His exceptional skills won him a place on the West Indies team. Coming to England in 1923, he played professionally for nine years from 1929 in the Lancashire League.

Constantine was a member of Harold Moody's League of Coloured People and an advocate for racial equality in Britain. In 1943 he and his family were refused pre-booked accommodation at a London hotel on the grounds of their race. He sued, winning his case and damages. The incident raised the issue of racism in the public eye, highlighting the colour bar that operated in the UK.

During the Second World War, Constantine worked for the Ministry of Labour overseeing the welfare of West Indian workers. He was awarded an MBE in 1945. In his book *Colour Bar* (1954) he criticised racism within sport and British society. After returning to Trinidad in 1954 and working within politics, Constantine came back to London in 1961 as Trinidad and Tobago's High Commissioner and was active in securing the country's independence in 1962. He was made a life peer in 1969, becoming the first person of African descent to sit in the House of Lords. Constantine died in 1971 and was given a state funeral in Trinidad, followed later in the same month by a memorial service at Westminster Abbey.

An English Heritage plaque was erected at this address in 2013 to commemorate him.

ELISABETH WELCH

SINGER, ACTRESS (1904-2003)

Flat 1 Ovington Court, Ovington Gardens, SW3 1LB

Elisabeth Welch was born in New York in 1904 and came to London in the 1930s. Her mother was Scottish, and her father was part black, part native American. Associated with great black entertainers, including Josephine Baker, Adelaide Hall and Bill 'Bojangles' Robinson, she launched the Charleston dance on Broadway prior to coming to London.

In 1931 Welch popularised Cole Porter's song 'Love for Sale' (which was banned from radio for many years) in the Broadway hit *The New Yorkers*, and in 1933, she introduced the famous song 'Stormy Weather' to British audiences. She also starred in two films with Paul Robeson in the 1930s. Subsequently, in 1934, she became the first black broadcaster to have her own BBC radio series, called *Soft Lights and Sweet Music*. After her death in 2003 it was discovered that Elisabeth had had an affair with the newspaper heir David Astor in the 1930s but their relationship never became public and ended when his formidable mother Nancy Astor intervened.

A plaque was unveiled at Ovington Court, Kensington – the building where Welch lived for over seventy years – by the African American critic and author Bonnie Greer in 2012. She is the second black woman to be honoured with an English Heritage plaque in the city, the first being Mary Seacole.

CLAUDIA JONES

ACTIVIST (1915-64)

The Tabernacle, 34–35 Powis Square, Notting Hill, W11 2AY

Claudia Jones was born Claudia Vera Cumberbatch in Trinidad in 1915. In the 1940s her parents moved to the USA looking for a better life, but by the time she was old enough, Claudia realised there wasn't a better life in America, so she joined the American Communist Party. In 1955 the American government deported her to England, where she immediately joined the UK's Communist Party and set up one of the first newspapers aimed at black people: the *West Indian Gazette*. The paper was used by Claudia to inform black people of

A Tribute to Notting Hill Carnival Pioneers

Europe's largest multicultural festival takes place on the streets of West London every August Bank Holiday weekend. The roots of Carnival b as an artistic expression by people from Africa and its Diaspora celebrati emancipation. The Notting Hill Carnival is a re-interpretation of Trinidad's c that evolved from the political and artistic resistance to colonization.

Integrated framework for Notting Hill Carnival involves live performances in 'F 1) Mas 2) Steel Pan 3) Calypso & Soca 4) Static Sound Systems 5) Mobile Sour

The 70 names highlighted on this plaque include: Carnival Committee Admin Steel Band Leaders, Pan People, Mas Band Leaders, Costume Designers and So ey are a small, but important, representation of the countless individuals (espec helped to shape and create the history, tradition and legacy of Notting Hil

* Claudia Jones
* Rhaune Laslette
* Russell Henderson
* Sterling Betancourt
* Leslie 'Teacher' Palmer
* Selwyn Baptiste
* Merle Major
* Lawrence Noel
* Andre Shervington
* Pearl Conner
* John Hopkins

* Junior Telfer
* Granville Pryce
* Victor Critchlow
* Anthony Perry
* Robert 'Bigger' Hamilton
* Tony Soares
* Bertha Joseph
* Vijay Ramlal Rai
* Alex Pascal
* Claire Holder
* Ali Pretty
* Ralph Cherrie
* Peter Joseph
* Pedro Burgess
* Randolph Baptiste
* Ashton 'Tailor' Charles
* Peter Minshall

* Arthur Peters
* Silma Faustine
* Rocky Byron
* Vernon 'Fellows' Williams
* Larry Forde
* Ansel Wong
* Clary Salandy
* Dexter Khan
* Michael La Rose
* Nikki Lyons
* Philmore 'Boots' Davidson
* Clive 'Mash up' Phillips
* Tony 'Cowboy' Charles
* Gerald Forsythe
* Pepe Francis
* Frank Rollock

* Joyce Bacchus
* Carlton 'Zigilee' Constantin
* Theo Stevens
* Ralph Richardson
* Desmond Bowen
* Emmanuel 'Eman' Thorpe
* Gloria Cummins
* Wilfred Walker
* Brian Henderson
* Ezekiel 'Biggs' Yearwoo
* Aubrey Bryan
* Cyril Khamai
* Corinne Skinner Cart
* Basil 'Black Patch' Jar
* Bernice McNaughton
* Sir Coxsone

✷ and to the innumerable carnival contributors, volunteers, stewards stall holders, revellers, radio DJs and friends who helped to develop and establish the Notting Hill Carnival -

Thank You!

current news around the world, as well as to showcase art and culture.

In 1959 a black man from Antigua named Kelso Cochrane was murdered in London by white hooligans. This brought the racial tensions that had been festering in Notting Hill to the fore. Claudia saw this as an opportunity to unite the black community and, with the help of others, she arranged a Caribbean-style event, albeit indoors, in St Pancras Town Hall, Kings Cross. This is often cited as the forerunner of today's Notting Hill Carnival. In 1964, on Christmas Eve, Claudia suffered a heart attack and passed away peacefully at her home in Brixton. She was buried just to the left of the grave of Karl Marx, her hero, in Highgate Cemetery.

Claudia has three Nubian Jak plaques in Notting Hill; a bronze plaque is at Carnival Village, Powis Square, and two blue ones can be seen at Portobello Road (see map reference 13) and Tavistock Square. She also featured on a Royal Mail stamp celebrating Women of Distinction in 2008.

NOTTING HILL CARNIVAL
EVENT (1964)
Tavistock Square and Portobello Road, W11

The first ever Notting Hill Carnival was staged in the 1960s and was broadcast live on BBC Television. Held in St Pancras Town Hall, it was an indoor event for many years, but grew so large that it moved to become a two-day street festival in the Notting Hill area. At the time, this area was heavily populated by people who had migrated from the Caribbean and they had experienced increasing racial tensions.

The carnival aimed to bring cultures together in a positive way. Ultimately, it is a celebration of emancipation from slavery expressed through music, costume and culture. The Notting Hill Carnival has grown to be the largest carnival of its kind in Europe, with over 2 million people attending each year.

On 24 August 2018 the world's largest blue plaque was unveiled by the Nubian Jak Community Trust on Portobello Green. The names mentioned on this plaque are all associated with the Notting Hill Carnival. Claudia Jones was one of its founders (see p. 89), while Rhaune Laslett-O'Brien and Leslie Palmer developed the event into the outdoor street festival we know today. The decision to honour 70 pioneers on the giant plaque was significant, as it marked the 70th anniversary of the Windrush generation arriving in the UK from the Caribbean.

ARTHUR STANLEY WINT
RAF PILOT, OLYMPIAN, DOCTOR AND DIPLOMAT (1920-92)

22 Philbeach Gardens, Earl's Court, SW5 9DY

Arthur Stanley Wint was born into a middle-class family in Jamaica. A natural sprinter, at the age of 17 he was already named 'Boy athlete of the Year' and competing internationally. When the Second World War started, the Royal Air Force began recruiting in the colonies, and Wint and his two brothers joined up. He gained his wings in 1944 and saw active service as a Spitfire pilot.

After the war, in 1947, he won a scholarship to train as a doctor and left the RAF, completing his first year as a medical student at St Bartholomew's Hospital, London. In 1948 the post-war Olympic Games were held at Wembley Stadium and Jamaica participated for the first time. Wint headed the team and won silver in the 800 metres and Jamaica's first Olympic gold medal in the 400 meters. He qualified as a doctor in 1953 and was awarded an MBE in 1954. In 1955 he returned to Jamaica, where, in 1973, he was awarded the Jamaican Order of Distinction. From 1974 to 1978 he served as Jamaica's High Commissioner back in England, but his last years were spent in Jamaica before his death in 1992. A Nubian Jak plaque was erected at this address in 2012 in his memory.

KELSO COCHRANE
CARPENTER (1927-59)

36 Goldborne Road, North Kensington, W10 5PR

Born in Antigua, Kelso Cochrane was working as a carpenter in London when he was murdered by a gang of white men on the streets of Ladbroke Grove in 1959. He was 32 years old. The murder highlighted the hostility and racism that was rife in the area and endemic to Britain at the time. Many landlords, shops and establishments displayed signs saying: 'No Irish, No Coloureds, No Dogs'. History marks the murder as the first racially motivated killing in London after the Windrush generation migrated to Britain, but the police at the time treated it as a robbery gone wrong. The views of fascist politician Oswald Mosley were supported by a vocal minority and had led to riots in 1958.

Black people suffered violent attacks from 'Teddy Boys' both on the streets and in their homes. The attacks only stopped when they started resisting. On the night of his murder, Cochrane was walking home from Paddington General Hospital after suffering an injury at work. He was set upon by between four and six men, one of whom stabbed him with a stiletto blade. Although there were witnesses to the attack, none came forward. Cochrane's brother, Stanley, attempted to reopen the case in 2003, but to no avail. No one has ever been charged with Kelso's murder.

A Nubian Jak plaque was unveiled at Goldborne Road in 2009 by the Mayor of Kensington and Chelsea. The paper-maiche portrait pictured below was produced by Toby Laurent-Belson for the event, and a mosaic portrait by local artist Alfonso Santana was dedicated to him at the same time. Kelso Place in Kensington is named after Kelso Cochrane.

BOB MARLEY

JAMAICAN SINGER-SONGWRITER (1945–81)
42 Oakley Street, SW3 5QQ

O ne of the most globally acclaimed performers of reggae music, singer-songwriter and musician Robert Nesta Marley was born in Jamaica, but spent many years in London, arriving there initially at the request of fellow musician Johnny Nash, another popular reggae singer at that time. They played at Peckham Manor School, Cator Street.

Marley subsequently returned to Jamaica, where he converted to Rastafari, but in 1977, following political upheaval and an assassination attempt in Jamaica, he made his way back to London. In the same year he was also diagnosed with cancer. An ardent football fan, Marley reportedly regularly played with friends at both Battersea and Kennington Park, the latter being next to a Rastafarian temple in St Agnes Place that Marley visited in the late 1970s. In 1978 Marley made a video at the Keskidee Centre in Islington, for his hit song 'Is this Love?' The recording featured some of the local children. Following his death in 1981, he received a state funeral in Jamaica and the Order of Merit (OM) honorary award. Additional London plaques to Bob Marley and the Wailers were unveiled in 2012 and 2019.

There are two commemorative plaques to Marley in London. The first was erected in 2006 by the Nubian Jak Community Trust at 34 Ridgmount Gardens, Camden, where Marley stayed when he first came to London in 1972. In 2019 English Heritage unveiled a second here, at his former house in Oakley Road, Chelsea. A mural of Marley was commissioned in 2015 to replace one that had been destroyed during work on a new housing development. The vibrant image shown here was created by street artist Dale Grimshaw on the wall behind the Brockley Barge pub, 184 Brockley Road, Brockley, SE4 2RR (see p. 178). Bob Marley Way in Lambeth is also named after the singer. See also Bob Marley and the Wailers, p 96.

BOB MARLEY & THE WAILERS

REGGAE BAND

8–10 Basing Street, Notting Hill, W11 1ET

Bob Marley and the Wailers came together as a band in Jamaica in the early 1960s. Their sound came from the early Ska records of the time. By 1966 the line-up had gone from a sextet to a trio of Marley, Peter Tosh and Bunny Wailer. Prior to Marley's death, the band toured various countries singing such hit songs as 'Could You Be Loved' to 'No, Woman, No Cry', to name but a few. Their last UK concert in 1980 at the Crystal Palace Bowl concluded with the seminal 'Redemption Song'. After the death of Marley in 1981, the Wailers continued to play reggae music.

Three plaques commemorate the reggae royalty of Bob Marley & the Wailers. A Federation of Reggae Music plaque was installed in 2012 at 15 The Circle, Neasden, Brent, NW2 7QX where the band stayed while they were touring with singer Johnny Nash. In October 2019 a Nubian Jak plaque was unveiled here in Basing Street, Notting Hill, on the site of the old Island Record Studios building where the group had recorded the infamous album Exodus, voted the best album of the twentieth century.

The final Nubian Jak plaque was unveiled near the open-air stage in Crystal Palace Park, SE19 2BA, in October 2020, to coincide with Black History Month. The plaque was organised in collaboration with Bromley Council, Friends of Crystal Palace Park and its Trust. The special design features a regular blue plaque ringed with the Rastafarian colours of red, yellow and green. Red symbolises the bloodshed throughout history in the fight for black liberation, yellow the wealth of the African continent (particularly its gold), and green vegetation and hope for the promised land of Africa. This trio of colours was first used by Marcus Garvey's Universal Negro Improvement Association (UNIA) back in the early 1900s.

Bob Marley is also commemorated in London as an individual artist, see p. 95.

JOHN ARCHER
POLITICIAN AND CIVIL RIGHTS CAMPAIGNER (1863–1932)
55 Brynmaer Road, Battersea, SW11 4EN

John Archer was born in Liverpool to a Barbadian ship steward and an Irish mother. He travelled widely and while in Canada met Margaret, a black woman who became his first wife. Archer was a member of the African Association formed in 1897 by students all over the world. A supporter of African self-rule, he attended the first Pan-African Conference in London's

Westminster Hall in 1900 alongside founders Henry Sylvester Williams and John Alcindor. Archer worked in local politics and was voted onto Battersea Borough Council in 1906. In 1913, on becoming the first black Mayor of a London borough, he declared in his acceptance speech that he hoped his success would have a positive impact throughout the 'coloured nations' of the world. He was chosen as President of the African Progress Union in 1918. A lifelong activist for social and racial equality, Archer died in 1932 following a short illness.

John Archer has two plaques in Battersea. The first was erected by the Nubian Jak Community Trust in 2010 at Battersea Park Road, where Archer ran a photography shop. English Heritage unveiled in 2013 the one shown here at this house, where he lived for 20 years. In 2013 Archer also featured on a 'Great Britons' stamp set commissioned by the Royal Mail.

KHADAMBI ASALACHE
WRITER AND ARTIST (1935–2006)
575 Wandsworth Road, SW8 3JD

Number 575 Wandsworth Road was the south London home of Khadambi Asalache, a civil servant and writer, who was born in Kenya in 1935. The small plain exterior houses a distinctly embellished interior containing elaborate carved fretwork. Asalache studied art in

Europe and came to London in 1960. He bought the house in 1981 and over a 19-year period transformed it into a work of art.

Asalache initially started wood crafting to help disguise recurring damp in the building, and went on to decorate nearly all the surfaces as well as making furniture using reclaimed wood. His inspiration drew on his childhood and his travels, and combines a fusion of African, Islamic and British design. The house contains hand-painted African wall scenes and collections of beautiful and functional objects. During his career, Asalache taught, worked for the BBC African Service, and wrote poetry and novels. His book, *The Calabash of Life*, was published in 1967. Later, he became a civil servant at the Treasury and also served on the management council of the Africa Centre. Although a non-smoker, he died of lung cancer in 2006. He bequeathed his house to the National Trust and since 2009 it has been opened for pre-booked guided tours.

FURTHER AFIELD

141 COLDERSHAW ROAD
HOME OF ERIC AND JESSICA HUNTLEY
141 Coldershaw Road, Ealing, W13 9DX

A Nubian Jak plaque, unveiled in October 2018, celebrates the work of community activists and educators, Eric and Jessica Huntley (see p. 62), who lived at this address from 1909-10.

CESAR PICTON
COAL MERCHANT AND GENTLEMAN (c.1755–1836)
52 High Street, Kingston upon Thames, KT1 1HN

Cesar Picton is said to have been born in Senegal around 1755. Kidnapped as a six-year-old, he was given as a present after his abduction to the rich Phillipps family, along with a parakeet and a duck! The family owned Pembrokeshire Castle as well as property in Norbiton. Picton was brought up in Surbiton, and although originally a Muslim, was baptised as a Christian in 1762.

When his owner, Lady Philipps, died, she left Picton £100, and later her daughters would also bequeath money to him, demonstrating how well thought of he was by the family. With Lady Philipps' death, the family sold their home at Norbiton Place and her daughters moved to Hampton Court. Picton made good use of his inheritance, purchasing first a home and then a coal merchant company. The business did very well, and he became extremely rich and fat! Despite his wealth he never became involved with the abolitionist movement, although he was a contemporary of Ignatius Sancho. He died in 1836 and is buried in All Saints Church in Kingston.

A black plaque was installed by the Royal Kingston Borough here at 52 High Street, the house where Cesar Picton lived from 1788 until 1807. A blue plaque, installed by the local Residents' Association, can be found at his house in Thames Ditton, where he lived from 1816 until his death in 1836.

HAILE SELASSIE I
EMPEROR AND POLITICIAN (1892-1975)
Cannizaro Park, Wimbledon, SW19 4UE

Haile Selassie I was born on 23 July 1892 in Ethiopia. Crowned the country's emperor in 1930, he unsuccessfully appealed in 1936 to the League of Nations to support him against the Italian fascist invasion of his country; they gave him no assistance.

After being exiled from Ethiopia by the Italian invaders, he arrived in Wimbledon in 1937, where he took refuge with the Seligman family, who were active campaigners against British appeasement of the Italian invasion. Selassie was restored as emperor in 1941, with support from Britain, but in 1973 Ethiopia suffered a famine, followed by a military coup a year later. Selassie was imprisoned and died in 1975 after an operation. He was 83 years old.

This bust of Haile Selassie was unveiled in 1937. It was sculpted by Hilda Seligman, and stood in the Seligmans' garden, Lincoln House, in Wimbledon, until the property was demolished in 1957. It was then moved to Cannizaro Park, Wimbledon. After being restored, it was formally unveiled by the Mayor of Merton in October 2005. The ceremony was attended by a group of Rastafarians, members of the Seligman family, and relatives of the late emperor himself. In June 2020 the bust was smashed to bits by a group of Ethiopians when

they heard that a popular singer from that country had been killed by Ethiopian police. It no longer exists.

DAPHNE ADRIANA STEELE
NURSE (1929–2004)
Former St James Hospital, Balham, SW12

Daphne Steele was born in 1929 in the Dutch colony of Essequibo (now part of Guyana) as the eldest of nine children. Her father was a pharmacist, and her mother a housewife. In 1945, aged 16, Daphne started training as a nurse and midwife at the public hospital in Georgetown, before immigrating to the UK in 1951 to start a training programme at St James' Hospital in Balham.

Her career took her to the US in 1955 where she worked as a nurse for five years, before returning to work in the NHS, first in Oxfordshire and then in Manchester, where she became a deputy matron of a nursing home. She subsequently became head matron at St Winifred's Hospital in Ilkley, West Yorkshire. This was the first time a black person had been appointed as a matron anywhere in the NHS. The appointment made news worldwide, with Steele receiving around 350 letters from well-wishers. After the hospital closed in 1971, Steele became a health visitor at Leeds University. She died in 2004.

A Nubian Jak plaque was unveiled in October 2018 at the one-time site of St James' Hospital, where Daphne Steele had trained. More than a hundred people attended the unveiling ceremony, including her sisters Carmen and June, who spoke passionately about their sibling and the work she did.

STEVE BIKO
SOUTH AFRICAN ANTI-APARTHEID ACTIVIST (1946-77)
Steve Biko Way, Hounslow, TW3 3ED

This street is named after Steve Biko who was murdered by the South African police in 1977. He has several streets named after him in London, including Steven Biko Road, near to the Arsenal football stadium in Islington, and Steve Biko Lane in Sydenham.

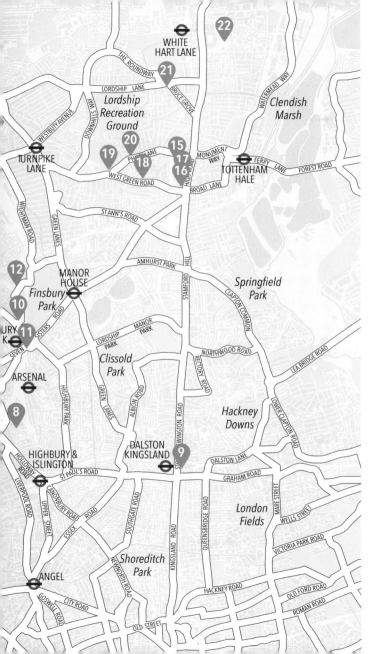

1. LORD DAVID PITT
2. ASQUITH XAVIER
3. CRANLEIGH STREET
4. LESLIE 'HUTCH' HUTCHINSON
5. PAUL ROBESON
6. KWAME NKRUMAH
7. DIDO BELLE
8. THIERRY HENRY
9. HIP HOP RAISED ME
10. GEORGE PADMORE & NEW BEACON BOOKS
11. JAZZIE B
12. LAURIE CUNNINGHAM
13. CY GRANT
14. EMMA CLARKE
15. MARCUS GARVEY
16. CYNTHIA JARRETT
17. BERNIE GRANT
18. DYKE & DRYDEN
19. WINDRUSH MEMORIAL
20. NICOLA ADAMS
21. BALTHAZAR SANCHEZ
22. WALTER TULL
23. OLIVER TAMBO
24. ALEXANDRA PALACE MURALS

3

NORTH LONDON

The second biggest population in the heavily multicultural area of Tottenham is the African and Caribbean community, a very large black contingent supporting the Tottenham Hotspur football team. When the *HMT Empire Windrush* arrived from the Caribbean in 1948, the area's housing was cheap and accessible, and people were able to find flats to rent, decent jobs and schools for their children. Since then, riots, high unemployment and high poverty rates have led to the area becoming run down in parts.

Other parts of north London include Camden and Islington. The ANC chose to set up its headquarters in the Borough of Islington in the 1970s, but unfortunately the South African police saw fit to bomb the building in the 1980s. Claudia Jones chose Camden as the venue for the first ever Caribbean carnival in London, which would later lead to the start of the Notting Hill Carnival.

LORD DAVID PITT
POLITICIAN, GP AND POLITICAL ACTIVIST (1913-94)
200 North Gower Street, NW1 2LY

David Pitt was born and raised in Grenada. In 1933 he won a medical scholarship to study at the University of Edinburgh, where he became a member of the Socialist Society. After graduating, he returned to the Caribbean and practised medicine in Trinidad, before becoming a founding member of the West Indian National Party in 1943, acting as its president until 1947. The party lobbied for self-government and constitutional reforms, and Trinidad was finally granted universal adult suffrage by the British Parliament in 1945.

Pitt returned to the UK in 1947 and opened a medical practice in Euston, which he ran for more than 30 years. Although unsuccessful in his political candidature for Hampstead in 1959, he went on to campaign against discrimination and helped to improve race relations. He was one of the founders of the Campaign Against Racial Discrimination (CARD) and served as the first Chair. Pitt was active in the anti-apartheid movement in South Africa and the campaign for Nuclear Disarmament. In 1961 he was elected to the London County Council and in 1974 he became the first black chair of the later Greater London Council. He was granted a life peerage in 1975. Pitt died in London in 1994 and was buried in Grenada with full honours.

The London Borough plaque at this address was unveiled in May 2000.

ASQUITH XAVIER
CIVIL RIGHTS ACTIVIST, TRAIN GUARD (1920-80)
Euston Station concourse, NW1 2DU

Asquith Xavier came to the UK from the Caribbean island of Dominica just after the war as part of the Windrush generation, most of whom came on the *HMT Empire Windrush*. This was a period when England needed to bolster its workforce and appealed to its former colonies to come and help rebuild the country. Asquith started work as a station porter at Marylebone Station and worked his way up to train guard. However, in 1966, after 10 years' service, he applied for another train guard position at Euston Station as the pay was much higher and he was supporting a family. When he was rejected in a letter that stated he did not get the job because Euston Station did not employ 'coloured' men in such positions, Xavier immediately protested about this hidden 'colour bar'. He took his case to Mrs Barbara Castle, who was then Minister of Transport, and in the same year the unofficial policy was overturned. Xavier was given the promotion he had previously been denied.

The Network Rail metal plaque commemorating the first non-white train guard in the UK hangs in the station concourse of Euston Station. Erected in 2016 to mark the 50th anniversary of Xavier's courageous stand against racial discrimination, it was unveiled in a simple ceremony attended by, among others, Asquith's family and Network Rail staff. In September 2020 a new plaque was unveiled at Platform 1 at Chatham Station where Asquith lived before he died. It was attended by RMT General Secretary Mick Cash and Asquith's daughter Maria Xavier.

22 CRANLEIGH STREET
HOME OF GEORGE PADMORE
Cranleigh Street Camden, NW1 1BD

A Nubian Jak plaque at this address celebrates George Padmore, renowned international activist and Pan-Africanist, who lived here from 1941-57. See p. 112.

LESLIE 'HUTCH' HUTCHINSON
SINGER AND PIANIST (1900-69)
31 Steele's Road, Chalk Farm, NW3 4RE

Leslie 'Hutch' Hutchinson was born in Grenada in 1900 and learnt to play the piano as a child. In 1916, he moved to New York, planning to study to be a doctor, but when he arrived, he found work instead playing the piano and singing in bars. Forgetting about his studies, he joined a band led by Henry 'Broadway' Jones that would often play to white millionaires such as the Vanderbilts. However, this brought the band to the attention of the Ku Klux Klan, who made their life a misery. Hutch left New York and went to Paris in 1924. There he met many people, including Cole Porter, who became his lover. By 1927 he was in the UK, where he met Edwina Mountbatten, who also became his lover. Between the 1920s and 1930s, he was one of the biggest stars in the UK, singing hit songs such as 'These Foolish Things', 'Begin the

Beguine' and 'Let's Do It, Let's Fall in Love'.

While married to Ella Byrd, with one daughter together, he fathered seven other children with multiple partners. One British debutant was found to be pregnant: her family married her off to a white officer but when it was discovered that the child was of mixed parentage, he divorced her and the child was given up for adoption.

Suffering from ill-health in his later years, Hutchinson eventually fell out of favour and died of pneumonia in 1969. Lord Mountbatten, Edwina's husband, paid for his funeral. He is buried in Highgate Cemetery.

The English Heritage plaque at this address was unveiled in 2012 by actor and author Stephen Fry and Hutchinson's daughter, Gabrielle Markes. In 2016 a BBC History Project plaque was unveiled to him outside Quaglino's restaurant in Kensington, where he performed.

PAUL ROBESON

SINGER, ACTOR, ACTIVIST (1898–1976)
The Chestnuts, Branch Hill, Hampstead, NW3 7NA

Paul Leroy Robeson was born in New Jersey, USA, the son of an escaped slave. He studied Law at Columbia University, where he was a star of the football team. When racism shut him out from the legal profession, he turned to the stage, and his big break came with playing Othello in London in 1930. However, the later knowledge of his affair with white actress star Peggy Ashcroft did not go down well with white audiences. Robeson had one of his biggest hits when he appeared in the film *Showboat*; singing 'Ol' Man River', he stole the show. This subsequently became his theme song wherever he went.

While living in London he studied at the School of Oriental and African Studies (SOAS). There he learnt to speak several African and other languages. A huge star in the UK, and Wales in particular, Robeson was a communist sympathiser, and a well-known star in Russia, especially after he was believed to have joined the Communist Party, although he was never officially identified as a member.

He returned to the USA in 1939 and spoke openly about the injustice black people had to suffer in the USA, and endured hardship himself during the McCarthy years in America when his passport was revoked and anyone who supported the Soviet Communist regime was seen as a danger to the country. In 1958 his passport was finally returned, and he toured Russia, where he became a leading figure in the struggle against fascism, colonialism and racism. However, by this time, his health was beginning to fail, and despite completing more world tours, he died in obscurity in 1976. An English Heritage plaque was erected at this address in 2002.

KWAME NKRUMAH
STATESMAN (1909–72)
60 Burghley Road, Camden, NW5 1UH

The first president of Ghana, Kwame Nkrumah was born in the then Gold Coast (now Ghana). He worked as a teacher, before living and studying first in the US and then in London in 1945. In the same year he helped to organise the fifth Pan-African Congress in Manchester, which consolidated resistance to British colonialism.

Nkrumah returned to the Gold Coast in 1947 as general secretary of the United Gold Coast Convention, which rallied and mobilised anti-colonial resistance deploying non-violent civil disobedience and strikes. Later, in 1950, he headed the Convention People's Party (CPP), calling for self-determination. He and other members were arrested by the colonial authorities and imprisoned, but in 1951 the CPP won a landslide victory. Nkrumah was released and became the party leader, going on to guide the Gold Coast (the first African colony) to independence in 1957. He also strengthened links within the African continent and reached out to its diasporas in the UK and USA. In 1966 his leadership was ended by a military coup and he died of cancer in 1972. An English Heritage plaque was erected at this address in 2005.

DIDO BELLE
GENTLEWOMAN (1761–1804)
Hampstead Lane, Highgate, NW3 7JR

Dido Belle was the illegitimate daughter of Sir John Lindsay and an African woman named Maria Belle. She was the cousin of Lady Elizabeth Murray, and the two women were both brought up at Kenwood by Mansfield and his wife, who were childless. Belle was baptised in London in 1766 and raised in this aristocratic family. The transatlantic slave trade was at its height in Georgian society and Lord Mansfield presided over landmark court cases in regard to British slavery: the Somerset case (1772), which made it illegal to transport slaves out of England; and the Zong case (1781), concerning live slaves who had been thrown overboard from a British ship, subsequent insurance claims being made for the loss of property. In his will of 1793, as well as leaving Belle an annuity, Mansfield declared her a free woman. She later married a steward (a senior servant), had children and lived in Pimlico until she died in 1804 aged 43. The film *Belle* released in 2013 by director Amma Asante dramatises Dido's life.

The original portrait of these two young women – in which only the white female, Lady Elizabeth Murray, was originally named – is attributed to the artist Johann Zoffany and resides at Scone Palace, Scotland. A copy of the canvas can be viewed at Kenwood House, north London, where it was painted. The estate at Hampstead Heath and dome of St Paul's Cathedral appear in the background. It was commissioned in the late 1770s or early 1780s by Sir John Lindsay's nephew, William Murray, the first Lord Mansfield and Lord Chief Justice from 1756 to 1788.

THIERRY HENRY
FOOTBALLER (b.1977)

Arsenal Emirates Football Stadium, Hornsey Road, N7 7AJ

Thierry Henry was born in 1977 in France; his parents originally came from Guadalupe in the Caribbean. He signed for Juventus from AS Monaco in 1999, and then, in the same year, for Arsenal, where – under the mentorship of coach Arsène Wenger – he developed into a prolific striker and world-class player, going on to become Arsenal's all-time leading scorer with 228 goals in all competitions. Henry won the Premier League Golden Boot four times, and his many other accolades include PFA Players' Player of the Year twice, and Football Writers'

Association Footballer of the Year three times. He won two FA Cup medals, two league titles as well as the 2006 UEFA Champions League.

Regarded as one of the best football players in the world, in 2007 he transferred to Barcelona, where he remained until 2010. He retired in 2014 and worked as a football coach for CF Montreal until February 2021 when he decided to leave for family reasons. Henry began coaching Arsenal's youth teams in February 2015, in tandem with his work for Sky Sports. Having earned a UEFA Licence, he was offered the job of under-18 coach by Academy head Andries Jonker, but the decision was overruled by Wenger, who wanted a full-time coach for the team.

On 10 December 2011, Arsenal unveiled a bronze statue of Thierry Henry at the Emirates Stadium as part of its 125th anniversary celebrations. It sits near to the turnstiles at the stadium. The statue is modelled on Henry's famous celebration of skidding on his knees after scoring a wonder goal against Tottenham Hotspur at Highbury in November 2002. The work was designed by MDM, the model- and prop-making company.

HIP HOP RAISED ME
CARLEEN DE SÖZER (2017)
Winchester Place, Dalston, E8 2PJ

The mural, *Hip Hop Raised Me* was created in 2017 by Carleen De Sözer, who often uses the colour gold in her designs. It is displayed in Winchester Place in Dalston, Hackney, very close to Ridley Road Market, one of the most popular markets in north London. Created in homage to her childhood heroes, the piece features some of the most well-known American hip hop artists of the 1980s and 90s, including Queen Latifah, Big Daddy Kane, and LL Cool J.

De Sözer was born in the late 1970s in Birmingham and is widely regarded as one of London's most skilled street artists. She has found a place on the international street art scene with her highly appealing Afrocentric and Afrofuturistic works. Carleen's work can be seen across London and internationally. Her most popular murals include *Golden Utopia*, *You Have the Keys*, *Golden Era* and *Grime Lords*. She also painted the Alexandra Palace Mural that pays homage to three pioneering black British women (see p. 128).

GEORGE PADMORE
PAN-AFRICANIST (1903-59)
George Padmore Institute, 76 Stroud
Green Road, Finsbury Park, N4 3EN

George Padmore was born in Trinidad and worked as a journalist before moving to the USA in 1924 to study Political Science and Law. He joined the Communist Party and abandoned his studies to organise black trade unions. Padmore moved to the Soviet Union in 1929 and was appointed head of the International Trade Union Committee of Negro Workers in 1930.

In his post he was able to forge links with African colonial countries and develop anti-colonial strategies. However, leading up to Second World War, the USSR's line on African colonialism changed and a disillusioned Padmore resigned.

He returned to London, where his home became a centre for anti-colonial activists from around the world, including Dr Kwame Nkrumah. It was also the place where he organised a campaign of opposition to

British colonial policies and planned the fifth Pan-African Congress held in 1945. In 1957 Ghana became the first African country to gain independence and Padmore moved there to take up the post of advisor to President Nkrumah. Caribbean writer C. L. R. James described Padmore as 'the father of African emancipation'. In 1959, following a short illness, Padmore died in London.

A Nubian Jak plaque was unveiled in 2011 at 22 Cranleigh Street, Camden, the former home of Padmore (see map reference 3). The George Padmore Institute is situated above the New Beacon Bookshop. Founded in 1991, it is small archive and research centre.

NEW BEACON BOOKS
PUBLISHER AND BOOKSELLER (1966)
76 Stroud Green Road, Finsbury Park, N4 3EN

New Beacon Books – the UK's first black publisher, specialist bookshop and international book distributor – was founded in 1966 by John La Rose and his partner Sarah White. Based in Finsbury Park, the bookshop sells books from Africa, the Caribbean, Asia, America, Europe, South America and Britain.

New Beacon as a publishing house has produced an important body of publications, including Bernard Coard's polemical *How the West Indian Child is made Educationally Sub-normal in the British School System* (1971). The bookshop has been at the centre of many ground-breaking political and social projects, organisations and campaigns, such as the George Padmore and Albertina Sylvester Supplementary Schools, the Caribbean Artists Movement (1966–72), and the Black Parents Movement (1975–80s). The George Padmore Institute is based above the shop, which celebrated its 50th birthday in 2016. It closed temporarily to reorganise under the New Beacon Development Group and reopened in 2017.

JAZZIE B
SINGER (b.1963)
Finsbury Park Station, Station Place, Finsbury Park, N4 2DH

Trevor Beresford Romeo, aka Jazzie B, 'the funky dread', is a DJ music producer, entrepreneur and the founding member of Soul II Soul. Born to Antiguan parents in Hornsey, north London, he ran sound systems – a collective of DJs, engineers and MCs – in partnership with his siblings during the 1970s. He had his first gig in 1977 and in 1982 the musical collective Soul II Soul was formed. Its motto was: 'a happy face, a thumping bass for a loving race'. From 1988 the band held a regular Sunday-night residency at the African Centre in Covent Garden before moving south to a larger venue, the Fridge.

The band's original sound and musical style combined British, Caribbean, African and African American influences. In 1989 their song 'Back to Life (However Do You Want Me)' charted at No. 1 in the UK singles charts. The band also topped the UK album charts and won a Grammy Award. Jazzie B is seen as the founding father of the British dance movement in the late 1980s, and in 2008 he received an OBE.

This steel statue pictured overleaf was unveiled in 2013 and can be found just outside Finsbury Park Station. It was set up by the Sustrans charity, which encourages people to travel by foot, bike or public transport. A Performing Rights Society (PRS) plaque can also be found at the Town Hall Parade, Brixton, at the Electric nightclub (formerly the Fridge) where Soul II Soul gave their first live performance.

LAURIE CUNNINGHAM
FOOTBALLER (1956–89)
73 Lancaster Road, Stroud Green, N4 4PL

Born of Jamaican parentage, Cunningham began playing football from an early age. Rejected by Arsenal, he was taken on by Leyton Orient Football Club in 1974. Then, in 1977, he joined West Bromwich Albion, where he played alongside Brendan Batson and Cyrille Regis, the three of them becoming known as 'the Three Degrees' after the American soul group. In total he won six caps representing England.

While at West Bromwich Albion he took part in one of the strangest ever football matches. It was a benefit match for Len Cantello and all the players were picked solely on their skin colour: black versus white. The black team won. It was the first – and so far last – football match to be played based solely on skin colour.

The second black player to don an England shirt, Cunningham was also the first black player to play for Real Madrid, who in 1979 paid the princely sum of £950K to acquire his services. Plagued by injury throughout his career, in 1989 he was about to hang up his boots when he was tragically killed in a car crash in Madrid, aged only 33.

Cunningham is one of those rare black people to have at least two plaques to commemorate them. The English Heritage plaque is on his home in Stroud Green, Finsbury Park, where he was bought up, and the Nubian Jak plaque is at Brisbane Road, home of his first club, Leyton Orient. In 2017, a statue of him was put up in Coronation Gardens,

Leyton, close to the same ground, and in 2019, the so-called Celebration statue of the Three Degrees – Cunningham and his colleagues Brendan Batson and Cyrille Regis – was put up outside the ground of West Bromwich Albion.

CY GRANT

RAF NAVIGATOR, SINGER, ACTOR AND CIVIL RIGHTS ACTIVIST (1919–2010)
54 Jackson's Lane, Highgate, N6 5SX

Cy Grant was born in Guyana and came to the UK in the 1940s when he joined the RAF as a navigator. In 1943, on his third operation, he was shot down over the Netherlands and taken as a POW by the Germans, who held him for two years until his release in 1945. After the war, Grant trained as a barrister, but despite his qualifications he was unable to find work so he turned to acting. After deciding to include

singing in his repertoire, he became a success on radio and TV. As well as having his own TV series in 1956 – *For Members Only*, in which he interviewed a variety of newsworthy people – he was asked in 1957 to feature in the BBC's daily topical programme *Tonight*, to sing the news in a calypso style – a role he remained in for two and half years. Between 1967 and 1968 he voiced the character of Lieutenant Green in Gerry Anderson's *Captain Scarlet and the Mysterons*, the first black character to appear in such a programme. In 1974, along with other creative colleagues, he set up the Drum Arts Centre in London: one of the first centres to focus on establishing a national centre for the arts of black people. Grant died aged 90 in 2010.

This Nubian Jak plaque was erected in November 2017, placed on the house where Cy Grant lived in Highgate. The event was attended by the Mayor of Haringey, Councillor Stephen Mann, Grant's former showbusiness contemporaries, and his family and friends.

EMMA CLARKE
FOOTBALLER (b.1871)
Campsbourne Primary School, Nightingale Lane, Hornsey, N8 7AF

Emma Clarke was born in Plumstead in 1871 to John and Caroline Clarke – one of 10 siblings. The first known black women's footballer in Britain, she was described by the *South Wales Daily News* as 'the fleet footed dark girl on the right wing'. A women's match held at the home of Crouch End FC in 1895 attracted over ten thousand supporters, and in 1897 she played for a women's team that had been specially put together called 'The New Woman and Ten of Her Lady Friends'. Their opponents were a male team called 'The Eleven Gentlemen', the ladies winning 3–1. Emma's sister, Florence, also played in that match. It's thought that Clarke's career as a footballer continued up to at least 1903, when she hung up her boots. There are no records of her life after this time, nor of her death.

A Nubian Jak plaque was unveiled at Campsbourne Primary School on 2 December 2019, which would have been Emma Clarke's birthday. The school is the site of the former Crouch End FC, the club for which Emma and her sister, Florence, once played. A girl's football tournament called the Emma Clarke Gold Cup was also launched on the same day.

MARCUS GARVEY
FREEDOM FIGHTER AND ACTIVIST (1887–1940)
1 Philip Lane, Tottenham, N15 4JA

Marcus Mosiah Garvey was born in 1887 in Jamaica. He was a political leader as well as a publisher, activist, journalist and entrepreneur. A fervent believer in black nationalism and Pan-Africanism, he promoted the return of black people to Africa. In 1914 he founded both the Universal Negro Improvement Association (UNIA) and the African Communities League (ACL). UNIA had over two million members. As Director of UNIA and ACL, Garvey set up various businesses to help the black community, his initiatives including the publication of a weekly newspaper called *Negro World* and the setting up of a shipping line, comprising four ships.

Both his first and second wives were called Amy, and both were influential and supportive of him in his aims. Garvey suffered a stroke

THE MARCUS GARVEY LIBRARY
THIS FOUNDATION STONE WAS LAID BY
MARCUS GARVEY JNR
7TH AUGUST 1987

IT COMMEMORATES THE CENTENARY OF THE LIFE
AND WORKS OF THE RIGHT HONOURABLE
BROTHER MARCUS MOSIAH GARVEY
THE AFRIKAN BORN IN JAMAICA W.I. ON 17TH AUGUST 1887
THE PEOPLE OF HARINGEY AND INDEED THROUGHOUT THE
WORLD HONOUR HIS LIFE COMMITMENT TO HIS PEOPLE IN
REGENERATING BLACK PRIDE SELF RELIANCE AND CONFIDENCE

in London in January 1940, aged 52, that left him all but paralysed, and six months later he died after a second. As the Second World War was raging at the time, he was interred in Kensal Green cemetery, but his body was eventually repatriated to Jamaica in 1964, where he was declared Jamaica's first national hero.

The Honourable Marcus Mosiah Garvey has the same bust in two different places. One (shown on previous page) is in the Marcus Garvey Library in Tottenham, unveiled in 1987. The other is in north-west London at the Willesden Green Library, 95 High Road, NW10 2SF, and was unveiled in 2016. The sculptor is unknown.

CYNTHIA JARRETT

MOTHER (1936–85)
Tottenham Town Hall, Tottenham, N15 4RY

Cynthia Jarrett was born on 26 July 1936, in the parish of Clarendon, Jamaica. She and her husband, known as Boysie, grew up together in the same area. Boysie came to the UK first and then sent for her to join him. Cynthia, whose nickname was Miss Dings, had a passion for fashion and loved glamorous film stars. She died of heart failure after police burst into her home in 1985, seeking evidence against her son, Floyd, who they had arrested earlier that day on the grounds of an allegedly suspicious tax disc. Her death sparked outrage against the Metropolitan Police, and led to the Tottenham Uprisings of 1985, during which a policeman, PC Blakelock, was murdered on the Broadwater Farm estate where Cynthia had lived. There was widespread belief that the police were institutionally racist – the week before, another woman, Cherry Groce, had been shot by police in Brixton. After the riots, and during the trial, Cynthia's daughter, Patricia, stated that she had seen the police push her mother, causing her to fall over. The police denied this had happened. No officers were charged and her death was deemed to be accidental. Three men were arrested for the death of PC Blakelock and sentenced to life imprisonment, but were subsequently released.

This tombstone can be found outside Tottenham Town Hall, Tottenham, where it was placed by Cynthia's family after her death. The granite plaque is etched in gold with Cynthia's name and reads 'symbol of the community'.

BERNIE GRANT
POLITICIAN (1944-2000)
Bernie Grant Arts Centre, Town Hall Approach Road,
Tottenham Green, N15 4RX

17

Bernie Grant was born in Georgetown, Guyana, in 1944, both his parents working in education. He arrived in England in 1963 and went to Tottenham Technical College, before going on to study engineering at Heriot-Watt University, Scotland. Starting his political life as a trade union official, he became a Labour Councillor in Haringey in 1978.

In 1985 he became the first black leader of a council in the UK. In the same year he came to national prominence dealing with the Broadwater Farm Estate uprisings and defending the young black people against police harassment. Two years later, Grant became one of the first black MPs to take his seat, entering the House of Commons on the opening of Parliament, fully clad in African attire. He served over 15 years in office and used his political platform to fight not only for racial justice, but also for an equal and fair society for all. On 8 April 2000, he died of a heart attack, age 56.

A bronze bust statue was unveiled in 2007. It was created by sculptor Christie Nicholas and is placed in the reception area of the Bernie

Grant Arts Centre which was designed by architect Sir David Adjaye OBE. In 2012, a Nubian Jak plaque was erected outside Tottenham Town Hall.

DYKE & DRYDEN

BEAUTY AND HAIR PRODUCT MANUFACTURERS (1965–90)

126 West Green Road, Tottenham, N15 5AA

Len Dyke and Dudley Dryden sold records and cosmetics in Ridley Road Market, Hackney, but when their friend Tony Wade joined the venture, he recommended that they put the record business aside and focus on black hair and skin products, as this was the way forward. Despite Wade joining the company, it was always known as Dyke & Dryden.

The venture saw the trio enjoy amazing growth, opening outlets in London and Birmingham, and partnering with local chemists. To add to their success, they launched the Afro Hair & Beauty Expo in the 1980s and created beauty contests and travel services for a growing black market. Dyke and Dryden imported black hair and skin products from the USA, where the leading suppliers could be found at the time, and went on to create the first perm hair curling gel ever formulated, which was developed in the UK under the name 'Super Supreme Curl'. They also developed a relaxing system (a cream which chemically processes afro hair) for the 'straight look', which got off the ground when Soft Sheen products of Chicago bought a controlling interest in the company. The trio even began selling a must-have accessory of the 1970s, the afro comb – a symbol of pride for the black community. Dyke, Dryden and Wade eventually sold up and retired in the 1990s, becoming the first black multi-millionaires in the UK.

A Nubian Jak plaque can be found on the former wig and cosmetic shop in West Green Road, Tottenham. It was unveiled by Rudy Page, an ex-member of the company, in November 2020.

WINDRUSH MEMORIAL
MEMORIAL (1998)
West Green Common, Tottenham, N15 5DA

The mass migration of Commonwealth citizens followed the introduction of the British Nationality Act 1948, which sought to ease Britain's unskilled labour shortage. Passengers on the *HMT Empire Windrush* (see p. 10) included a total of 1,027 passengers, including two stowaways. Many were ex-servicemen and people who had been invited to fill positions in the service industries, such as the London Underground and the NHS.

In 1998 Haringey Council unveiled this Windrush standing memorial plaque at West Green Common, Tottenham. It marked 50 years since the *Windrush's* arrival. Two rose bushes were planted alongside the plaque in 2018 to commemorate the 70th anniversary. The inscription on the plaque reads: 'This rose garden is dedicated to the people from the Caribbean who settled in Haringey'.

The plaque was the first memorial dedicated to Caribbean settlers in the area. Sadly, 2018 saw the Windrush scandal, with its 'hostile environment' and misplaced deportations. The following year saw the first national Windrush Day (22 June; see p. 26) and discussions for a permanent memorial to the Windrush generation.

NICOLA ADAMS
BOXER (b.1982)
Downhills Park, Downhills Park Road, West Green, N17 6PD

Nicola Adams was born in Leeds in 1982. Introduced to boxing by her father, Innocent Adams, who regularly showed her fights between Muhammad Ali and Joe Frazier – the 'Rumble in the Jungle' in particular – she asked her mother at the age of 10 to take her to the local boxing club, where, although she was the only girl, she beat everyone she fought against. Her first official fight was in 1996, but she did not win any awards until she was 17. In 2007 she made her international debut, representing Great Britain at the European Amateur Championships in Denmark. In August 2009, the International Olympic Committee added women's boxing to their events and Nicola was chosen to represent Great Britain. She won gold medals at the 2012 Olympics and the Commonwealth Games in 2014. In 2013 she was awarded an OBE and in 2017 her biography *Believe* was published.

This statue, representing the first female boxer to win an Olympic gold medal, was installed by the charity group Sustrans, which has erected a series of steel figures across the UK. The statues are chosen by locals to represent people from their community. Nicola is one of a set of three figures – the others are Walter Tull (see opposite) and Luke Howard – that can be found in Downhills Park, Tottenham. She also featured on a 2012 Royal Mail Olympic stamp.

BALTHAZAR SANCHEZ
SWEETMAKER (d.1602)
Bruce Castle Museum, Lordship Lane, Tottenham, N17 8NU

When King Philip of Spain arrived in England in 1554, he brought his servants with him. Sanchez was a Muslim and served the king making sweetmeats and other delicacies for him to enjoy. When Philip decided to return to Spain, Sanchez and his family remained, having taken a liking to England. They converted to Christianity and continued successfully producing their confectionery. They made enough money to buy land in Tottenham. When Sanchez died in 1602, he left sufficient funds in his will to ensure that more almshouses could be built for the poor of Tottenham. The almshouses remained *in situ* until 1923, when the buildings were demolished to create Burgess's department store, which was eventually demolished in the 1980s. Today, a supermarket stands on the site.

The plaque found here at Bruce Castle Museum is the only reminder of Balthazar Sanchez. It is made of wood and carries the Sanchez family crest.

WALTER TULL
FOOTBALLER AND SOLDIER (1888-1918)
77 Northumberland Park, N17 0TH

Walter Daniel John Tull was one of the first black footballers in the UK. His father – a carpenter – came from Barbados and his mother from Kent. When Walter was nine years old, both his parents died, leaving him and his brother as orphans. His love of football and talent for the game soon saw him playing for the Bethnal Green orphanage team, and in 1908 he signed for Clapton FC, then, in the next year, after being spotted by a scout, for Tottenham Hotspur, where he stayed until 1911. When the First World War started in 1914, he enrolled in the Footballers Battalion and was sent to train as a soldier in the army. He saw action in Italy and was recommended for the Military Cross, but there is no record of him ever receiving one. In 1918 Tull was sent to the front at the Somme, where he was killed in action. His body was never recovered.

The Nubian Jak plaque was erected in Tull's memory on 21 October 2014 at the house which now stands where he lived prior to the war, at 77 Northumberland Park, Haringey. The Walter Tull statue, which shows him wearing his football kit, was unveiled in 2007 and is one of three steel figures in Downhills Park, Tottenham. It was chosen by members of the local community to say who they think best represents their community. The other two statues are of Olympic Champion boxer Nicola Adams and 'father of meteorology', Luke Howard. In 2018 Tull also featured in a Royal Mail First World War stamp collection.

OLIVER TAMBO

FREEDOM FIGHTER (1917–93)

Albert Road Recreation Ground, Muswell Hill, N22 7XL

Oliver Tambo, Nelson Mandela and Walter Sisulu were the founding members of the African National Congress (ANC, see p. 73) and Youth Leagues in 1943. Tambo – a teacher and lawyer – became the first National Secretary of the ANC and, in 1948, a member of the National Executive. By 1958 he had become the Deputy President, but in 1959 he received a five-year banning order from the South African government. With his wife, Adelaide, he moved to England, and for the next 30 years, the couple and their family lived in London, Adelaide working for the NHS as a nurse. Finally, in 1990, they both returned to South Africa, the house there where they lived now being owned by the South African government.

The role Tambo played as the ANC's figurehead in Europe was vital in publicising the plight of black South Africans and canvassing international support for the fight against the white-minority apartheid government. Tambo died in April 1993 in Johannesburg from complications after a stroke. In 2006 the Johannesburg International Airport (formerly Jan Smuts Airport) was renamed after him. His wife

went on to become an MP in South Africa, supporting women's and disabled people's rights.

Sculpted by Ian Walters and unveiled in October 2007, this bronze bust statue can be found close to Tambo's house, where there is also a plaque to commemorate his time in north London. It was unveiled by Zanele Mbeki, the wife of South African president Thabo Mbeki.

A later statue of Tambo was unveiled in October 2019 by South African High Commissioner to the UK, Her Excellency Thembi Tambo, who is Oliver Tambo's daughter and lived with him in Haringey. The statue is made of bronze, is 1.7 meters (5.5ft) tall and was commissioned by the Oliver Tambo Memorial Working Group. Attendees at the unveiling included Lord Boateng, the first ever black British High Commissioner to South Africa; former South African High Commissioner, Lindiwe Mabuza; and representatives from the Cameroonian, Sudanese and Namibian High Commissions.

ALEXANDRA PALACE MURALS
MURAL (2018)
Alexandra Palace, Alexandra Palace Way, N22 7AY

This mural features three iconic black women: Winifred Atwell, Evelyn Dove and Una Marson. They can be viewed on the south side wall of Alexandra Palace, Wood Green. The artwork was created by street artist Carleen De Sözer in 2018 as part of London Mayor Sadiq Khan's year-long campaign for women's equality called 'LDN WMN: Behind Every Great City'. This drive marked a century since women in the UK won the right to vote and was undertaken in partnership with the London Tate Collective.

The three women are each inspirational in their own right and together changed entertainment in Britain. From left to right, they are:
– Winifred Atwell (1914–83) was a Trinidadian pianist. The first black woman to have a number one record in the UK – in 1954, with 'Let's Have Another Party' – during her lifetime she sold over 20 million records.
– Evelyn Dove (1902–87) was born in the UK to a Sierra Leonean father and English mother. She was a powerful singer and actress of the 1940s and 50s.
– Una Marson (1905–65) was born in Jamaica and was the first black female to have her own show on BBC Radio in the 1940s. She has a London Borough plaque in Southwark.

Carleen De Sözer was born in Birmingham in the late 1970s. The renowned muralist also created *Hip Hop Raised Me* (2017) (see p. 112).

MENELIK ROAD
STREET
West Hampstead, NW2

This road is named after Menelik II, Emperor of Ethiopia from 1889 to 1913. The road was built on the estate of the Powell-Cotton family, Major Percy Powell-Cotton having been given permission by the Emperor to hunt in Ethiopia in 1900. The Powell-Cottons were a very well-off family. Major Percy Powell-Cotton was an English explorer, hunter and early conservationist. He travelled all over Africa searching out animals to hunt and kill. The animals he killed he brought back to England and put in his museum in Kent (the Powell-Cotton Museum) which is still there to this day. It is said he has the largest number of game ever shot by any person.

FURTHER AFIELD

DENNIS BROWN
MUSICIAN (1957–99)
55 Hazeldean Road, Harlesden, NW10 8QT

Dennis Brown was born in Jamaica and showed musical potential from an early age. His talent was noticed by the reggae music industry and in 1969, aged only 12, he released his first single, 'No Man is an Island', going on in 1977 to achieve a UK chart hit with 'Money in My Pocket'. He subsequently set up DEB Records in London, which married lovers rock with Third World sounds. His vast canon of work over the decades earned him an entry in the *Guinness Book of World Records* and worldwide status. Brown was Bob Marley's favourite singer, dubbed by him as 'The Crown Prince of Reggae'. Following a long-standing drug addiction, Brown died of pneumonia in 1999. Two years later, in 2011, he was posthumously awarded Jamaica's Order of Distinction for his contribution to the Jamaican music industry.

A Nubian Jak plaque was unveiled in 2012 at this address. His wife, brother and other members of the Brown family were present, along with notable guests including David Rodigan MBE. Collaborators in the erection of the plaque included the Jamaica High Commission and the Federation of Reggae Music.

GEORGE ALFRED BUSBY
GENERAL PRACTITIONER (1899–1980)
66 Erskine Road, Walthamstow, E17 6RZ

George Busby was born in Barbados in 1899, but six weeks later his family moved to Trinidad, where the rest of his siblings were born. A bright child, George earned a place at Queen's Royal College, developing a lifelong friendship with fellow pupil C. L. R. James, who was later to become a world-renowned historian.

In 1917, George won the coveted Island Scholarship, awarded on the results of the Higher Certificate Examination, entitling him to study at university in the UK. But that had to wait until after the First World War ended in 1919, when Busby finally made his way to the UK.

He went on to work as a GP in Walthamstow from 1926 to 1929, in the pre-National Health era when medical care was not free, and he often recalled the barter system by which the butcher paid him in pork chops. Dr Busby and his wife (a nurse) were committed to making a difference to healthcare in their community, and he continued interacting with his Walthamstow patients long after he left Britain by writing letters to them, and they responded by keeping him up to date about what was happening in the area. In 1929 he set sail for the Gold Coast, where he lived for the rest of his life. He died in 1980 aged 81.

A Nubian Jak plaque was unveiled at this address in March 2020. Attending the event were many of Dr Busby's family and friends, including his daughter Margaret Busby, who was the founder of the publishing house Allison & Busby (with Clive Allison).

1. HAROLD MOODY
2. FRANK BATES
3. PETE ROBINSON
4. THE DARK AND LIGHT THEATRE COMPANY
5. UNA MARSON
6. SAM KING
7. WALTER RODNEY
8. MARIANNE JEAN-BAPTISTE
9. RIO FERDINAND
10. DAMILOLA TAYLOR
11. PECKHAM PORTRAITS
12. THE BLACK CULTURAL ARCHIVES
12. MORANT BAY REBELLION
12. SHARPEVILLE MASSACRE
12. AFRICAN AND CARIBBEAN WAR MEMORIAL
13. C. L. R. JAMES
14. WINIFRED ATWELL
15. RUDY NARAYAN
16. CHERRY GROCE
17. OLIVE MORRIS
18. ROTIMI FANI-KAYODE
19. FIRST CHILD
20. CHILDREN AT PLAY
21. PLATFORM PIECE
22. BRONZE WOMAN
23. MICHELLE OBAMA
24. MICHAEL JOHN
25. 198

4

SOUTH LONDON

When the ship *HMT Empire Windrush* arrived in Tilbury in 1948, some of the Caribbean arrivals were temporarily housed in the Clapham South deep shelter in south-west London. The shelter was close to Brixton Labour Exchange and the majority of those looking for work would go to this exchange to see what was available. This led to an influx of people settling into the Brixton area, new arrivals staying with friends and family living there – so much so that it became the 'capital' for black people arriving from abroad, and is still seen as the centre of Black London. As well as being the place Nelson Mandela asked to visit in 1996, it is the location of The Black Cultural Archives and was home to the writer C. L. R. James and activist Olive Morris.

Southwark has a large black population in one of the most famous areas of London – Elephant and Castle. The famous insignia associated with this area was part of the Royal African company founded by the Duke of York in 1662, which shipped more African people to the Americas than any other institution in the Atlantic enslavement era. In the 1930s the borough was home to Harold Moody, who founded the League of Coloured Peoples. The arts are strongly represented in the borough, being the location for the Peckham Portraits, artworks and murals.

HAROLD MOODY
DOCTOR AND CAMPAIGNER FOR RACIAL EQUALITY (1882-1947)
Peckham Library, Peckham Hill Street, SE15 5JR

Harold Arundel Moody was born in Jamaica and travelled to England to study medicine at King's College London in 1904. He faced the colour bar in housing and securing employment. Nevertheless, in 1913 he qualified as a doctor, set up his own practice at his home in Peckham and married an English nurse. Later, in 1931, he founded the League of Coloured Peoples (LCP) with other middle-class black figures. Notable celebrities, including Paul Robeson and Kwame Nkumah, visited his home. Combining his medical and activism roles throughout his life, Dr Moody championed the social, economic, educational and political life of African and Caribbean people both in Britain and worldwide as well as challenging racial discrimination. He died in 1947 aged 64 and the LCP continued until 1951.

The bronze bust shown here was sculpted by Harold's brother, Ronald Moody, in 1946. It was purchased by Southwark Council in 2007 and is on permanent display at Peckham Library. A copy of the bust is also displayed at the National Portrait Gallery. In 1995 an English Heritage plaque was unveiled at Moody's former home in Queens Road, Peckham, and in 1999 the park on Gordon Road, Peckham, was also renamed after him. In 2019 the Nubian Jak Community Trust commemorated his work with a plaque at the Central YMCA, Great Russell Street (see Central London map ref 38), where Moody, a committed Christian, first sought help in finding accommodation.

FRANK BATES & PETE ROBINSON
MUSICIANS (1889-1921) & (1888-1921)
19 Hichisson Road, Peckham Rye, SE15 3AN
8 Crewdson Road, Oval, SW9 0LJ

Pete Robinson was born in the USA, Bates in Barbados. Later both serving in the British Merchant Marines, Bates was a vocalist and Robinson a drummer in the Southern Syncopated Orchestra (SSO). Both men spent time in London, married English partners and had children. The SSO – a 36-piece band of musicians and singers of African American, Caribbean, and British-born African heritage – was formed by

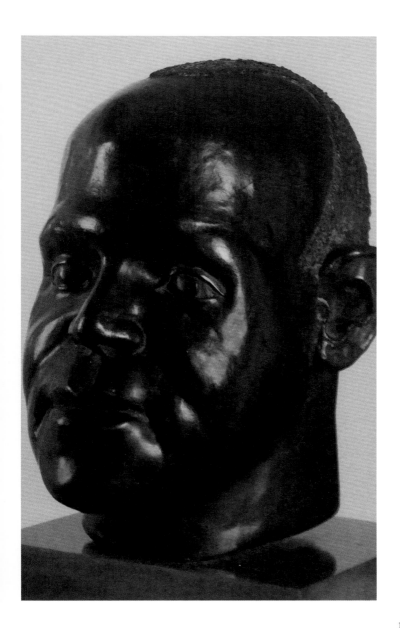

American composer Marion Cook. When it arrived in the UK in 1919 it was initially fronted by jazz pioneer Sidney Bechet. The orchestra at the time was at its height, and in the same year was not only invited to play at Buckingham Palace but also topped the bill at the Royal Festival Hall for the first anniversary of the armistice. Two years later, the orchestra was among the passengers on the steamship *SS Rowan*, en route from Glasgow to Dublin, when it collided with two other vessels. Thirty-five people lost their lives, including eight members of the SSO. Both Bates and Robinson died in the disaster, which made worldwide news at the time, coming nine years after the sinking of the *RMS Titanic* in 1912. The orchestra disbanded within the year.

These two Nubian Jak plaques at these addresses form part of a tribute to some of the illustrious musicians who played in the SSO. Both were unveiled in 2013; that for Frank Bates at 19 Hichisson Road, Peckham Rye, and for Pete Robinson at 8 Crewdson Road, Oval.

THE DARK AND LIGHT THEATRE COMPANY
THEATRE (1969–75)
Longfield Hall, Knatchbull Road, Camberwell, SE5 9QY

4

The Dark and Light Theatre Company (DLT) later called the Black Theatre of Brixton, was the first black-led ensemble in the UK. It showcased work by African and Caribbean writers, made all productions multicultural, and incorporated African storytelling such as the tale of Anansi the spider. The company also toured the UK and formed a local youth community theatre group. Yvonne Brewster directed the first Jamaican pantomime at the DLT and in 1986 she went on to be one of the founders of Talawa, the primary black theatre company in the UK, which is still going strong. Longfield Hall provides a space for a range of community activities, arts and theatre.

The Nubian Jak plaque shown here was unveiled in October 2019 to commemorate 50 years since the formation of the DLT. The

Grade-II-listed Longfield Hall housed the DLT group, which was founded in 1969 by Jamaican actor Frank Cousins. Cousins, celebrities and past members including Carmen Monroe and Rudolf Walker were in attendance for the unveiling. The plaque provides a permanent reminder of the DLT's history and its contribution to British theatre.

UNA MARSON

**POET, JOURNALIST, CIVIL RIGHTS ACTIVIST
AND BBC PROGRAMME MAKER (1905–65)**
16c Brunswick Park, Camberwell, SE5 7RJ

Una Maud Victoria Marson was born in Jamaica in 1905. After studying to be a secretary, she came to London in 1932, where she got a job working with the BBC Empire Service – the first black woman to do so. Prior to this she had been secretary to Marcus Garvey (see p. 118). She also worked as Assistant Secretary to Dr Harold Moody, founder of the League of Coloured Peoples (see p. 136).

In 1942 Marson became producer of the programme *Calling the West Indies*, which in turn became *Caribbean Voices*, an important forum for Caribbean literary work giving a platform to various black writers, poets and playwrights (such as Samuel Selvon) who would go on to become famous in their own right.

Marson herself was a skilled poet, writer and journalist, and used those skills to enhance her career. In 1936 she returned to Jamaica, where she helped to create the Kingston Readers & Writers Club as well as founding the Jamaica Save the Children Fund. Marson came back to London to continue her work before returning to Jamaica for the final time in 1965, and while there she died.

The London Borough plaque was unveiled at this address in 2009 by her biographer, Delia Jarrett-Macauley, whose book, *The Life of Una Marson 1905–1965*, was published in 1998. Marson also features in the Alexandra Palace Murals, north London (see p. 128).

SAM KING

COMMUNITY ACTIVIST AND POLITICIAN (1926–2016)

2 Warmington Road, Herne Hill, SE24 9LA

Sam King was born in Jamaica and in the Second World War and volunteered with the Royal Air Force, working as an engineer. He returned to London in 1948 aboard the *HMT Empire Windrush*.

King settled in Camberwell and worked for the Royal Mail for 34 years, starting as a postman and going on to become a manager. He was involved with Britain's first black newspaper, the *West Indian Gazette*, which was founded by Claudia Jones (see p. 89). King was also instrumental in organising the first Caribbean carnival that led eventually to the launch of the Notting Hill Carnival in 1964.

Involved in community activism, King joined the Labour Party in 1982, and in 1983 became Mayor of Southwark. With Arthur Torrington he set up the Windrush Foundation in 1995, a charitable and educational organisation aimed at keeping the legacy of this post-war generation alive. In 1998 he was awarded an MBE and also published his autobiography *Climbing Up the Rough Side of the Mountain*. King died in 2016 aged 90 and his funeral was held at Southwark Cathedral. A London Borough plaque was erected to King in 2011.

WALTER RODNEY
HISTORIAN, POLITICAL ACTIVIST AND ACADEMIC (1942–80)
Peckham Square, SE15 5RS

Born in British Guiana (now Guyana), Rodney studied in Jamaica and graduated in 1963, going on to study in London at the School for Oriental and African Studies, where he earned a PhD in African History in 1966. Travelling widely, he taught in universities in Tanzania and Jamaica. Rodney was a socialist, part of the Black Power Movement and an activist for change in the post-independence Caribbean, becoming a key figure in Caribbean radical politics in the 1960s and 70s. He joined others to object to the political direction of the government in Jamaica, which had gained its independence from Britain in 1962, and in 1968 he was banned from returning to the country and dismissed from his teaching post. This led to student riots in Jamaica that resulted in six deaths.

In 1972 his most influential book *How Europe Underdeveloped Africa* was published by the Huntley's Bogle L'Ouverture Publications. Rodney returned to Guyana in 1974 and founded the Working People's Alliance. In 1980, aged only 38, he was assassinated via a car bomb.

A Community Council plaque in Peckham Square (between Peckham Library and the swimming pool), was unveiled in 2005.

MARIANNE JEAN-BAPTISTE
ACTRESS (b.1967)
St Giles Road, Camberwell, SE5 7RN

Marianne Jean-Baptiste was born at the former St Giles' Hospital in Camberwell, now a residential block for the nursing school located there, and grew up in Peckham with an Antiguan mother and St Lucian father. After studying at the Royal Academy of Dramatic Art in London, she went on to work on both stage and screen. Overlooked at the British Screen's 50th anniversary in 1997, Jean-Baptiste was one of the first black actors to speak out against the lack of opportunity and diversity within the UK acting establishment.

The first black Briton to receive an Academy Award nomination (Best Supporting Actress) for the 1996 Mike Leigh film *Secrets and Lies*, which deals with issues of race and class and won the Palme d'Or at

Cannes, she went on in 1999 to play Doreen Lawrence in *The Murder of Stephen Lawrence*. In the same year she relocated to America to improve her work prospects, and she continues to live with her family in Los Angeles. She has appeared in various US TV dramas and films as well as returning to the British stage.

Southwark Council unveiled a London Borough plaque at this address to Jean-Baptiste in 2013.

RIO FERDINAND

FOOTBALLER (b.1978)

Friary Estate, Leyton Square, Peckham Park Road, SE15 6SX

Rio Ferdinand was born at King's College Hospital in Denmark Hill and grew up in Peckham. He attended Camelot Primary School and went on to Blackheath Bluecoat School. During his football career he played at West Ham United, Leeds United, Manchester United and QPR, his club transfers involving record-breaking fees. Ferdinand earned 81 England caps, played in three World Cups, and is one of the most decorated footballers of all time.

In 2012 he launched The Rio Ferdinand Foundation Charity, which aims to create opportunities for young people. The foundation runs informal sports sessions and provides mentoring on Southwark estates. In 2013 Ferdinand announced his retirement from international football. The former Premier League football hero is involved with TV and continues to be a spokesperson against racism in football.

In 2003 Southwark Council unveiled a plaque to Rio at the Friary Estate, Peckham. It is unusual in being one of the few plaques to commemorate a living person.

DAMILOLA TAYLOR

SCHOOLBOY (1989-2000)

Oliver Goldsmith Primary School, 83 Peckham Road, SE5 8UH

Damilola Taylor was born in Nigeria and had two siblings, one of whom suffered from a severe form of epilepsy. His mother and the children moved to London in the summer of 2000 to seek treatment for this condition. Damilola had only recently started at his new school when, in November, he set off home after his studies at Peckham

Library. Tragically, that was the last time he was seen alive, as he was violently attacked with a broken bottle by two teenage boys near his home. In 2001 his father Richard Taylor established the Damilola Taylor Trust in his son's memory. The Trust and its centre aim to support and inspire young people by providing activity programmes, sports, mentoring and a career pathway.

This Phoenix sculpture is a tribute to the memory of Damilola Taylor, whose young life was cut short after his senseless killing. Unveiled in 2002, the structure was created by student Alexandra Brooke in collaboration with Camberwell College of Arts. The bird symbolises hope rising out of tragedy. It stands on a pillar within the small garden at Oliver Goldsmith Primary School in Camberwell, facing out to Peckham Road.

PECKHAM PORTRAITS

PHOTOGRAPHS (2019)

Mountview Academy of Theatre Arts building,
120 Peckham Hill Street, SE15 5JT

The Peckham Portraits are a series of large-scale black-and-white photographs that celebrate the achievements of black British actors. The images were unveiled in 2019 as part of Black History Month celebrations and can be viewed on the Mountview Academy of Theatre Arts building in Peckham Hill Street. Franklyn Rodgers' photographs were initially shown in 2008 at the National Portrait Gallery and had a temporary location at the Peckham Plex cinema. The portraits were initiated by actor Fraser James of Underexposed Arts to present 'foundations of inspiration'.

The images of stars from stage and screen include Angela Wynter, David Oyelowo, Idris Elba, Marsha Thompson and Ashley Walters. Each portrait also features some words of wisdom beneath. Thompson's reads 'Embrace the chaos' and Walters' 'You can do what I've done but you've got to have that focus, you've got to have that plan.' Rodgers' distinctive works are exhibited internationally and are held in the permanent collections of the National Portrait Gallery, Tate Britain and Autograph.

THE BLACK CULTURAL ARCHIVES

ARCHIVES

Black Cultural Archives, Windrush Square, Brixton, SW2 1EF

Established in 1981, the Black Cultural Archives (BCA) is situated in Windrush Square, Brixton. Len Garrison, academic, community activist and co-founder of BCA, asked the question, 'Where are our Heroes, Martyrs and Monuments?' He catalogued the development of black British identity and his collection became the foundation of the archive. A bust of Garrison by the sculptor George 'Fowokan' Kelly takes pride of place inside the main reception. This national heritage centre opened in 2014 and is dedicated to collecting, preserving and celebrating the history and culture of African and Caribbean people in Britain.

The BCA houses an exhibition, archive and research facilities including a reading room and reference library, as well as a café and bookshop. Its collections include objects, documents, oral histories and publications. Among the archives is a small silver coin, dating from AD 208, depicting Septimius Severus, the black Roman emperor. In collaboration with Google Arts & Culture, the BCA has also digitised over four thousand items, forming a series of online exhibitions. Its aim is to promote the teaching and learning of Black British history through its exhibitions, public programmes and events.

MORANT BAY REBELLION
PLAQUE (1865)
Black Cultural Archives, Windrush Square, Brixton, SW2 1EF

This BBC History Project plaque was unveiled in 2016 and can be viewed at the entrance of the Black Cultural Archives in Brixton. It commemorates those who fought and were killed in one of the largest rebellions against British rule in Jamaica.

In 1670 Britain took control of Jamaica from the Spanish. The island played a fundamental part in the triangle slave trade, with the importation of Africans forced to work on the sugar plantations fuelling Britain's economic expansion. In 1831 Sam Sharp led a rebellion against enslavement, which was followed by 10 days of uprisings. Although, in theory, slavery had been abolished in 1807 and slaves were emancipated in 1834, the British still had total control over the black population. In the 1864 US election, most black males were excluded from voting.

The following year tensions exploded in the Morant Bay Rebellion, which started with a protest march to the courthouse led by the black Baptist preacher Paul Bogle in response to continuing injustice and poverty. Martial law was declared, and troops killed men, women and children indiscriminately. Thousands of homes were burnt and over six hundred people flogged. Like Sharp before him, Bogle, along with 14 others, was hanged. In 1969 he was named as one of Jamaica's National Heroes and his statue stands in Morant Bay.

SHARPEVILLE MASSACRE
MEMORIAL (1987)
Windrush Square, Brixton, SW2 1EF

In 1987 Lambeth Council unveiled this standing memorial to the Sharpeville Massacre. Attendees included the former council leader Linda Bellos and Archbishop Trevor Huddleston. The main plaque features an image of protesters on a map of Africa and the inscription reads 'They died so others may live'.

South Africa in the middle of the last century operated under an apartheid system of white minority rule and racial segregation. In 1960 Robert Sobukwe, a leader in the anti-apartheid Pan-Africanist Congress (PAC), organised a peaceful demonstration against restrictive pass laws in the Sharpeville suburb. Pass documents were used to control the movement of the black African majority. Thousands of protesters gathered at Sharpeville police station, where armed officers fired initial shots into the crowd to disperse them. As people attempted to flee, the shooting continued, with 186 shot in the back and 69 killed. Although the massacre awakened international attention and sparked further protests, the South African military regime continued its suppression, banning anti-apartheid groups such as the PAC and the African National Congress. Mass arrests ensued, including that of Sobukwe, who was imprisoned on Robben Island. After release, he faced restrictions on his liberty until his death in 1978.

AFRICAN AND CARIBBEAN WAR MEMORIAL
MEMORIAL (2017)
Windrush Square, Brixton, SW2 1EF

Devised by the Nubian Jak Community Trust, this memorial was unveiled on 22 June 2017 in Windrush Square. The monument stands in remembrance of more than 2 million African and Caribbean servicemen and women who participated and fought in both world wars. It also serves as a historical legacy for future generations. The memorial is formed of two 6-foot (1.8-metre) black stone obelisks, which rest on a 12-foot pyramid-shaped plinth, the structure in total weighing over 5 tonnes. The inscription lists the different services commemorated and ends with: 'And to all the Forgotten'.

As part of the Empire, many men and women volunteered and were also recruited to the war effort. The British West Indies Regiment was enacted by Army Order in 1916. Caribbean men served in the Royal Air Force and the Merchant Navy; Caribbean women in the Women's Auxiliary Air Force and Auxiliary Territorial Service. Fifty-five thousand men from Africa also served in the Labour Corps. Although they did not fight in Europe, they were deployed in the Middle East on the African continent.

Windrush Square in Brixton was renamed as such by then Mayor of London Boris Johnson in a ceremony in 2010 to commemorate the *HMT Empire Windrush*'s arrival at Tilbury Docks in 1948. It started life as Tate Library Gardens in 1905 when it was purchased by Jane Tate, the wife of Sir Henry Tate. A bust of Sir Henry still remains in the square as a reminder of its original name.

C. L. R. JAMES
WRITER AND POLITICAL ACTIVIST (1901–89)

165 Railton Road, Brixton, SE24 0JX

13

Cyril Lionel Robert James was born in Trinidad and came to England in 1932. A friend of fellow Trinidadians Sir Learie Constantine and George Padmore, he worked as a cricket reporter, as well as writing for left-wing journals, as an ardent anti-colonialist.

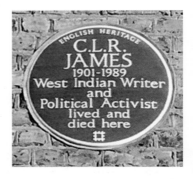

In 1936 he wrote a play about Toussaint L'Ouverture, the leader of the Haitian slave revolution. It was performed at Westminster Theatre, and starred the African American actor Paul Robeson (see p. 108). In 1938 James moved to the USA, where he published *The Black Jacobins*, a history of Haitian independence. He also wrote books on race, class and politics, as well as lecturing on political issues. After a period living in Africa, he returned to London in 1953. His book *Beyond a Boundary* (1963) was a study of politics and cricket as well as being his autobiography. In the 1980s James enjoyed iconic status and was awarded an Honorary Doctorate from South Bank Polytechnic (later to become the University of the South Bank) in London. His final eight years before his death in 1989 were spent in Brixton.

This English Heritage plaque was unveiled in 2004, and is located just above the Brixton Advice Centre. In 1985 Hackney Council renamed Dalston library the Dalston C. L. R. James Library, in James's honour.

WINIFRED ATWELL
PIANIST (1914–83)

82 Railton Rd, Brixton, London, SE24 0LD

 14

Una Winifred Atwell was born in Tunapuna, Trinidad and Tobago. A child prodigy, she studied the piano from the age of four. She met her husband-to-be, Lew Levishon, in London in 1945, and they married within a few months of meeting, Lew giving up his job as a comedian to become her manager. Atwell went on to have several firsts: first black female to have a number one hit record in the UK; first black female pianist to have shows on both ITV and BBC TV; first black female to sell a million records in the UK. She also went on to sell 3 million records, including another number one in 1956. Her most famous tune was the 'Black and White Rag', which was used as the soundtrack to the BBC TV series *Pot Black*.

In 1957 Atwell opened in Brixton what is thought to be the first black hairdressers in the UK. Upon visiting Australia in the 1950s, she fell in love with the country, and by the 1970s she and her husband had made it their permanent home. Levishon died in 1978 and Atwell never recovered from his death. She died in 1983 from a heart attack and is buried in Australia next to her husband.

A Nubian Jak plaque can be found on the side of Atwell's former hairdressing salon here in Railton Road, Brixton. It was one of the first erected as part of Nubian Jak's Black Plaque Project. The blue replacement plaque for Atwell was unveiled in December 2020.

RUDY NARAYAN

BARRISTER, CIVIL RIGHTS ACTIVIST AND COUNCILLOR (1938-98)
413 Brixton Road, SW9 7DG

R udy Narayan was born in Guyana in 1938 and came to the UK in 1953 with his family. In 1969 he founded the Afro-Asian and Caribbean Lawyers Association, which would later change its name to the Society of Black Lawyers. Specialising in trials involving black people and the police, he defended clients in 1981 such as the Bradford Twelve and many from the St Paul's riot in Bristol. Narayan's battles with the legal profession led to the creation of the Bar Council's race relations committee in 1984 and an amendment to the Race Relations Act to prohibit race discrimination in the legal profession.

In 1974 Narayan was elected as a Labour Party councillor for Lambeth Council and served one term. The BBC series *Black Silk*, which ran for a year from 1985, was loosely based on his life and work. Narayan was portrayed by actor Rudolph Walker. He died in 1994 of cirrhosis of the liver at King's College Hospital, Lambeth.

A Nubian Jak plaque was put up in conjunction with the Society of Black Lawyers in 2010. Narayan practised Law at this venue from 1987 until 1994. In attendance at the unveiling was His Excellency Laleshwar K. N. Singh, High Commissioner for Guyana, Councillor Neeraj Patil and the Mayor of Lambeth. Jak Beula, chair of the Nubian Jak Community Trust, was also present and spoke on the day.

CHERRY GROCE
MOTHER (1948–2011)
22 Normandy Road, Brixton, SW9 6JH

Cherry Dorothy Groce was born in Jamaica in 1948 and came to the UK in 1962. A mother of six, she was innocently shot in 1985 during a bungled police raid of her home. The shooting sparked the Brixton riot of that year. Groce was left paralysed and died from her injuries in 2011. In 2014 a jury inquest found that police failures contributed to her death.

Groce's son, Lee Lawrence, established the Cherry Groce Foundation in 2014 to honour the strength and spirit of his mother and also to help people deal with extraordinary life challenges. In 2020 he published his memoir, *The Louder I Will Sing*. The book takes its title from the 1987 hit song 'Something Inside So Strong' by black British singer-songwriter Labi Siffre.

A Cherry Tree Trust plaque was erected in 2012. A memorial designed by architect Sir David Adjaye OBE was due to be unveiled in 2020, but was delayed due to Covid-19. It will mark 35 years since the shooting. The Cherry Groce Memorial Pavilion in Windrush Square will include a covered seating area and is intended as a place of reflection and shelter. Lambeth Council funded the memorial alongside a contribution from the Metropolitan Police.

OLIVE MORRIS
CIVIL RIGHTS ACTIVIST (1952–79)
18 Brixton Hill, Brixton, SW2 1RD

Olive Elaine Morris was born in Jamaica and came to London as a child, going on to make significant contributions to black communities in both London and Manchester. Many political organisations were based in and around Brixton, and Morris – a leading member of the Brixton Black Women's Group, the British Black Panther Movement and the Organisation of African and Asian Descent Group – was an active fighter against racism, sexism and oppression. She was also instrumental in the campaign for squatter's rights and fought against the SUS law (police stop and search). She died prematurely from cancer aged just 27. The original organisation, Remembering Olive Collective, has now evolved into ROC 2.0 and aims to ensure her legacy of local activism lives on. The Olive Morris Collection of documents is held at Lambeth Archives.

In 2009 Morris was chosen by popular vote as one of the historical figures to feature on the Brixton Pound, a local community currency. Designed by artist Jeremy Deller, the notes celebrate local figures within the arts, politics and culture. From 1986 to 2019, the former Lambeth Council offices at 18 Brixton Hill were renamed Olive Morris House, the radical campaigner's contribution to the area being commemorated by a plaque inscribed with the words 'My heart will always be in Brixton'.

ROTIMI FANI-KAYODE
ARTIST (1955–89)
151 Railton Road, Brixton, SE24 0LT

Oluwarotimi (Rotimi) Adebiyi Wahab Fani-Kayode was born in Nigeria; his father was a politician and Yoruba chief. In 1966, aged 12, Rotimi came to the UK following the civil war in his country. He was privately educated in England and went on to graduate in Fine Arts and Economics at Georgetown University, then to postgraduate studies at the Pratt Institute in New York City, before returning to the UK in 1983.

Fani-Kayode's stylised photography expresses and asserts black male sexuality, race and identity. The male body is at the centre of his work exploring the relationship between erotic fantasy and ancestral spiritual values. In 1988 he, along with other members, co-founded the Association of Black Photographers (now named Autograph) in Brixton, Fani-Kayode serving as its first chair.

His influence spans 1980s black British art and continues into the twenty-first century, with his photographs forming part of the exhibition 'Masculinities: Liberation through Photography' at the Barbican Art Gallery in 2020. Fani-Kayode died in London of a heart attack while recovering from an AIDS-related illness. Many of his photographs were created in collaboration with his late partner Alex Hirst and are collected in the posthumous 1996 publication *Rotimi Fani-Kayode and Alex Hirst: Photographs*. A small golden plaque at 151 Railton Road, Brixton commemorates the life and work of the artist.

FIRST CHILD
MEMORIAL (1998)
Max Roach Park, Villa Road,
Brixton, SW9 7ND

The steel statue *First Child* was created by Jamaican artist Raymond Watson. Standing on the corner of Brixton Road and St John's Crescent in Max Roach Park, it was unveiled in June 1998. Within a week, it was reported that it had been wrecked by vandals. Luckily, it was restored and remains on public view.

The memorial is dedicated to the 116 black schoolchildren who were massacred by the South African police force in Soweto in 1976. The children were demonstrating against unfair schooling rules under the apartheid government. The piece is modelled on the photo of a 12-year-old boy who was shot and scooped up in the arms of Hector Pieterson. The picture, taken by a local journalist, went viral around the world.

Watson was born in 1958, in London, England. He later moved to the Caribbean. He has exhibited his sculptures as well as executed public commissions locally and overseas, and has participated in several exhibitions at the National Gallery of Jamaica. In 2007, he was inducted into the Hall of Fame of the Caribbean Foundation for the Arts.

CHILDREN AT PLAY
MURAL (1982)
Brixton Academy, Stockwell Park Walk, SW9 9SL

The *Children at Play* mural was created by artist Stephen Pusey in collaboration with Lambeth Council in 1982. Located on the back wall of the O2 Academy Brixton, on Stockwell Park Walk, it was produced after the Brixton riots erupted in 1981 and is the largest mural in the borough.

In the 1980s Brixton had high unemployment and crime, plus

increased racial tensions between a predominately white police force and black youths. Five days prior to the riot, the police had put 'Operation Swamp' into action, stopping and searching approximately one thousand black males. Three days of unrest occurred, which involved looting, violence and almost three hundred arrests. The inquiry into the riot produced the Scarman Report, which acknowledged racial disadvantage, negative policing and institutional racism.

Following the riots, discussions took place with residents of the Stockwell Park Estate to produce a permanent artwork within the community. The vibrant image of racial harmony between the playing children serves as a legacy to Brixton's multiracial neighbourhood.

PLATFORM PIECE
MURAL (1986)
Brixton Railway Station, Brixton, SW9 8HX

The three figures that form the work *Platform Piece* can be found at Brixton railway station. They are the work of Kevin Atherton, and were unveiled in 1986 by Sir Hugh Casson as part of a £1 million renovation of the overground station – a joint venture between British Rail and Lambeth Council.

The three life-size bronze effigies represent commuters of the 1980s. They were cast in bronze using the lost-wax process, an old African technique of casting statues. The two black models were Peter Lloyd and Joy Battick, who both worked at the station, and Karin Hestermann, a German woman who lived in the area. In November 2016 the statues were given listed Grade II status by Historic England. The Lloyd and Battick figures are believed to be the first ever listed sculptural representations of black figures in the UK.

BRONZE WOMAN
SCULPTURE (2008)
Stockwell Memorial Gardens, SW8 1UQ

This larger than life sculpture was unveiled in 2008 – the brainchild of Guyanese-born teacher, playwright and poet Cécile Nobrega, who wrote a poem of the same name. It took 10 years of planning, fund-raising and determination to complete the project. Originally, the statue – depicting a mother and baby – was due to be fashioned by Ian Walters, the same sculptor who designed the Nelson Mandela statue in Parliament Square. Unfortunately, Walters died before it could be finished, so a young sculptor named Aleix Barbart completed the work.

Bronze Woman represents the struggles faced by Caribbean women, as well as their contribution to British society. Nobrega, who came to London in 1969, was 89 years old when the statue was finally unveiled. She died in 2013. In June 2019 a Nubian Jak plaque was unveiled at Lee Samuel House (retirement housing) at 10 Nealden Street where Nobrega lived.

MICHELLE OBAMA
MURAL (2018)
Dorrell Place, Brixton, SW9 8EG

In 2018 the artist Dreph created murals of Michelle Obama and Michael John, both of which can be found in Brixton. This mural of Michelle Obama in Dorrell Place marked the release of her autobiography *Becoming* in 2018. Michelle topped Dreph's series of inspirational London portraits entitled 'You Are Enough'. The collection celebrated a range of women from creatives to educators making a positive difference in their communities. A champion for the education of girls, the former First Lady visited London in 2009 with her daughters and gave a motivational speech at the Elizabeth Garrett Anderson School in Islington.

Artist Neequaye Dreph Dsane is a former secondary school art teacher. His contemporary portraits present alternative narratives and highlight living unsung heroes and heroines. With over 30 years' experience of street-based painting, his diverse artworks grace walls in the UK and worldwide. In 2020 Dreph's work became a set feature in the BBC TV soap *EastEnders*. A large-scale mural depicting the face of a black female is displayed on the wall opposite the famous Queen Vic pub.

Fire exit
Keep clear

MICHAEL JOHN
MURAL (2017)
Pope's Road, Brixton, SW9 8PQ

Dreph's '*Migration*' collection was put together after Brexit and the national conversation around immigration. Michael John's portrait can be viewed in Pope's Road. John's image portrays one of the first generation of immigrants to have made the UK their home. He came from Grenada and is a long-standing member of the community. In 2016 John received the 'Keys to Brixton Market' from Lambeth council.

198
ART SPACE AND GALLERY
198 Railton Road, Brixton, SE24 0JT

The 198 Contemporary Arts and Learning space is a centre for visual arts, education and creative enterprise. It grew out of the social unrest of the 1980s in the Brixton area. The centre was behind a project that commissioned the first public sculpture by a black artist in the UK: *First Child*, by Jamaican artist Raymond Watson (see p.152). In October 2019, it launched the inaugural biannual Women of Colour Art Awards.

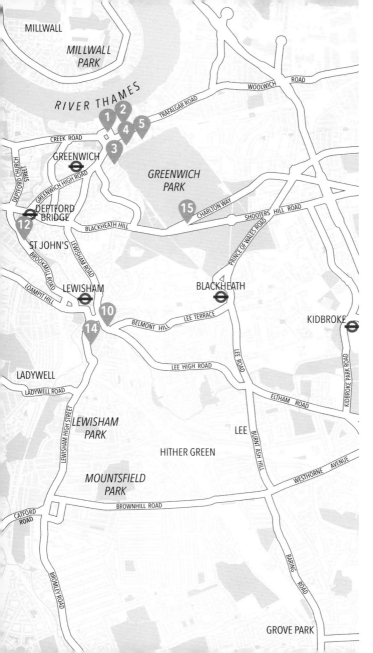

1. JOHN BLANKE

2. FELA KUTI

3. STEPHEN LAWRENCE GALLERY

4. NELSON'S SHIP IN A BOTTLE

5. THE SHIP OF FOOLS

6. GEORGE ROBERTS

7. NEW CROSS FIRE STATION

8. NEW CROSS FIRE MEMORIALS

9. THE BATTLE OF LEWISHAM

10. ASQUITH GIBBES

11. THE BROCKLEY BARGE PUB

12. STEPHEN LAWRENCE CENTRE

13. BLUE EARTH

14. THE MIGRATION MUSEUM

15. GREENWICH PARK

5

SOUTH-EAST LONDON

John Blanke is associated with Greenwich, as was Ignatius Sancho, who spent his early years as a servant in this area. Greenwich's neighbour, Deptford, was a slaving port from the fifteenth century onwards, and was where merchant John Hawkins had a base and operated from. It was at the Deptford docks that Olaudah Equiano was kidnapped and sold from one ship's captain to another. As many black people arrived in London by ship, there was a heavy population in those areas around the Thames. Black people mainly populated the area around Deptford, as it was close to the river, and the sailors could work on a ship if they were needed. The community expanded as time went by.

Ships docked in the area during the eighteenth and nineteenth century, bringing with them spices and accoutrements from all over the British Empire. The Empire was upheld by the navy with their base at the Old Royal Naval College, Greenwich. The maritime history of Greenwich is also reflected in the contemporary artworks *Nelson's Ship in a Bottle* and *Ship of Fools* (see p. 170-3).

As with Brixton, Lewisham also has a sizeable black population and likewise experienced racial tensions in the 1970s and 80s. This was marked by the black and white communities' battle against the right-wing National Front, and the tragedy of the New Cross Fire.

JOHN BLANKE

MUSICIAN (c.1500)

Old Royal Naval College Visitors Centre,
Greenwich, SE10 9NN

In February 1511 King Henry VIII held a two-day celebration to commemorate the birth of his short-lived son. The Westminster Tournament Roll depicts the king's joust. At approximately 60 feet long and 15 inches wide, it is held at The College of Arms in London and is not on public view. John Blanke appears twice on the roll in the procession to and from Westminster. The unnamed artist failed to change Blanke's hand colour on this second image, therefore it remains white though his face is black. Dressed formally in the royal livery, he stands out from the group of six mounted trumpeters with his green and gold turban. The presence of black musicians at European courts denoted prestige and is echoed in the artwork of the period. Blanke's image is the earliest of a named person of black origin in England and is one of the most requested pictures from the The College of Arms.

In 2016 the BBC programme *Black and British: A Forgotten History* commemorated key events and people through the unveiling of plaques across Britain, Africa and the Caribbean. John Blanke was one of the historic figures recognised. Then, in 2017, a BBC History Project plaque was erected at the Old Royal Naval College Visitors Centre, Greenwich. The centre was originally part of Greenwich Palace, the birthplace and favoured residence of Henry VIII.

Blanke may have arrived in England via Queen Katherine of Aragon's entourage. Court records show payments and garments issued to a 'John Blanke, the blacke trumpeter' and also document his successful petition for a pay rise. He married in January 1512 and the last mention of him is the note of wedding gifts from King Henry.

FELA KUTI
ENTERTAINER AND ACTIVIST (1938–97)
King Charles Court, Greenwich, SE10 9JF

Fela Kuti was born in Nigeria and as a young man was sent to London to study medicine. However, his interest in music led him to study composition and the trumpet at the then-named Trinity College of Music, now the Laban. Kuti formed a band called Koola Lobitos and they developed a style of music now known as Afrobeat, with influences from African 'highlife' to the Black Power movement.

His band was popular in London clubs and they toured in the USA. Kuti spent many years in London and recorded *Fela's London Scene* in 1971 at the famous Abbey Road Studios. Nigeria was a British colony from 1850 to 1960, and Kuti used his music to challenge the colonial legacy as well as the continual government corruption and political injustice that persistently served the minority. Kuti's views and lifestyle led to confrontational and controversial events, which included his house being burnt down by the Nigerian government, an 18-month imprisonment on trumped-up charges, and a mass 'marriage' to 27 of his female troupe. He died in 1977, allegedly from an AIDs-related illness. Kuti left a vast musical legacy that lives on with his sons.

This Nubian Jak plaque can be found at Trinity Laban Conservatoire of Music at King Charles Court, Greenwich. It was erected in November 2020, with attendees including Dele Sosimi, the musician and musical director for Fela Kuti's *Egypt 80* album. Kuti's son Femi and grandson Made sent a video message of thanks from Nigeria. Like his grandfather, Made Kuti also studied at the conservatoire.

STEPHEN LAWRENCE
TEENAGER (1974–93)
The Stephen Lawrence Gallery and Project Space,
10 Stockwell Street, SE10 9BD

In 1993 Stephen Lawrence was murdered in a racially motivated attack while waiting for a bus in Eltham, south-east London. A stone memorial is inlaid in the pavement at this final site. He was 18 years old and a promising student. The police failed to charge any suspects and his parents fought tirelessly to receive justice. In 1998 a private prosecution concluded that the police force was 'institutionally racist'. In the same year, the Stephen Lawrence Charitable Trust (later renamed 'Blueprint for All') was set up to promote a positive community legacy. In 2012, two of the original five perpetrators were finally convicted of murder, and on 22 April 2019 the first national Stephen Lawrence Day (see p. 26) was observed to commemorate his life.

A Nubian Jak plaque was unveiled in 2013 at the Stephen Lawrence Centre, Brookmill Road, Deptford. The painting *No Woman, No Cry* by artist Chris Ofili (see previous page) is a tribute to the London teenager and his family. It takes its title from the 1974 song by Bob Marley. The words 'R.I.P. Stephen Lawrence' are inscribed within the multi-layered artwork and his face is captured inside each of the tears shed.

The work was purchased in 1999 and can be viewed at Tate Britain, Millbank. The Stephen Lawrence Gallery had two previous homes within the University of Greenwich and since 2014 it has been based at its Stockwell Street site in the heart of Greenwich. The gallery aims to promote diversity in the representation of visual cultures. Doreen Lawrence was a former student at the university.

NELSON'S SHIP IN A BOTTLE
SCULPTURE (2010)
Greenwich Maritime Museum, SE10 9NF

This incredible monument was first displayed on the fourth plinth in London's Trafalgar Square during the period 2010–12, its creator, Yinka Shonibare MBE, being the first black artist to be commissioned to show there. Since 2012 the artwork has rested on a column at the entrance of the Greenwich Museum. It depicts a replica of Nelson's battleship *HMS Victory*, with the sails made of brightly coloured 'African' batik fabric. This material was inspired by Indonesian design, mass-produced by the Dutch and sold to the colonies in West Africa. Like many of Shonibare's works, the piece explores the tangled interrelationship between Africa and Europe. It is also a celebration of Britain's multicultural society. After Nelson's victory at the Battle of Trafalgar the seas were freed for the British to build their Empire; subsequently, individuals and families from countries within that Empire came to live in Britain.

Shonibare was born in London in 1962 and moved to Nigeria aged three. He returned to London to study Fine Art and completed his studies at Goldsmiths College. In 1980 he suffered from a spinal inflammation that resulted in partial paralysis. As an international artist he has works in London and collections worldwide. Elected a Royal Academician in 2013, Shonibare was awarded a CBE six years later, in 2019. He also created *The British Library* (see p. 68).

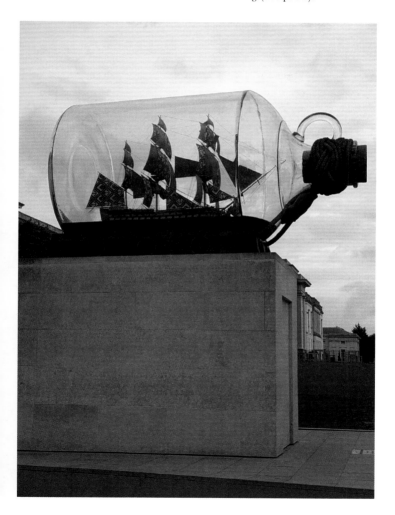

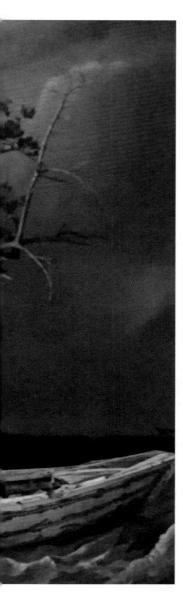

THE SHIP OF FOOLS
PAINTING (2017)
Queen's House, SE10 9NF

This painting of young black men at sea by African American artist Kehinde Wiley can be viewed at the Queen's House, National Maritime Museum in Greenwich. Inspired by a painting by Hieronymus Bosch of the same title, it is the first work by Wiley to be bought for a public collection in the UK. Wiley's contemporary canvas contrasts to the other maritime works of European exploration, conquest and power that in turn gave rise to slavery, genocide and colonialism. The portrait depicts the perilous journey thousands of immigrants and refugees endure at a time of closed borders.

Wiley is known for his large-scaled, vibrant patterned portraits depicting black people posing as famous figures in Western art. His paintings challenge the absence of black people from traditionally renowned art histories and also explore themes of race, identity and power, celebrating and creating a wider visual narrative. In 2018 Wiley was the first black American to be commissioned to paint the official presidential portrait of the 44th president, Barack Obama, which is on display at the Smithsonian National Gallery in Washington, DC.

GEORGE ROBERTS

SOLDIER, FIREMAN AND COMMUNITY LEADER (1890–1970)

Lewis Trust Dwellings, Warner Road, Camberwell, SE5 9LZ

George Roberts was born in Trinidad and trained as an electrician. He enlisted and fought in the First World War with the Middlesex Regiment. After the war he settled in south-east London and in 1931 joined the League of Coloured Peoples as one of the founder members alongside Dr Harold Moody. The organisation challenged discrimination and voiced the needs of the black community.

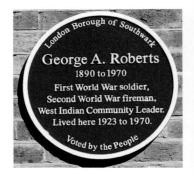

Roberts was too old for combat in the Second World War and joined up for the Home Front as a firefighter during the Blitz. He completed his training in 1939, was stationed at New Cross Fire Station and was promoted to Section Leader in 1943. In King George VI's 1944 Birthday Honours, Roberts was awarded the British Empire Medal for his pioneering work within the Fire Service. He also campaigned for ex-servicemen rights and founded his local British Legion. A portrait of Roberts in his uniform was painted by Norman Hepple, but its whereabouts are unknown. He died at King's College Hospital, London, in 1970.

In 2016 this London Borough plaque was unveiled to Roberts at the home where he lived for nearly 50 years. Firefighters formed a guard of honour at the ceremony and attendees included the Acting High Commissioner of Trinidad and Tobago.

He was also honoured with a London Fire Brigade plaque in 2018 at New Cross Fire Station. His great-granddaughter and representatives from the London Fire Brigade and the Fire Brigade's Union attended the unveiling.

NEW CROSS FIRE STATION
PLAQUE
266 Queen's Road, SE14 5JN

See George Roberts, opposite.

NEW CROSS FIRE MEMORIALS
MEMORIAL (1981)
Fordham Park, New Cross, SE14 6LU

The memorial stone in Fordham Park, New Cross, commemorates the victims of the 1981 New Cross Fire. It was installed in 2012 with a bench set opposite for people to sit and contemplate. The stone lists the 13 young black lives lost in the tragic house fire at a 16th birthday party (one survivor died two years later). A Nubian Jak plaque was put up with the support of Lewisham Borough Council on the house at 439 New Cross Road. The council also have a twin memorial plaque outside the entrance of the Civic Suite, Lewisham Town Hall.

After the fire, the indifference of the establishment and negative media coverage inspired writer Benjamin Zephaniah to pen the poem, '13 Dead, Nothing Said', which became a slogan for the justice campaign. There was a feeling that the young black lives that had been lost were not deemed to have the same level of value as the lives of white teenagers. On Monday 2 March 1981, 20,000 black people took part in a protest march named the Black People's Day of Action. It started from New Cross, and proceeded to Blackfriars Bridge, ending at Fleet Street. The call was for racial equality and justice. Two inquests into the fire recorded open verdicts.

THE BATTLE OF LEWISHAM
MURAL (1977)
323 New Cross Road, SE14 6AS

On 13 August 1977 the far-right National Front Party planned to march through New Cross to Lewisham. Anti-racist and anti-fascist organisations mobilised alongside the community, who took to the streets. On that morning, over 4,000 people from more than 80 organisations heard speeches by the Mayor of Lewisham and the Bishop of Southwark at a counter-demonstration in Ladywell Park. One of the key people at the event was Darcus Howe, civil liberties campaigner, one of the Mangrove Nine in 1970 and also a speaker on the day.

Protesters clashed with both the National Front and the police. The protest marked the first time a National Front march was prevented from reaching its destination, and also the first deployment of riot shields on the UK mainland. The rediscovered documentary *Aug 13: What Happened?* by the London Community Video Archive chronicles the events.

In August 2017 a London Borough plaque was unveiled at 323 Clifton Rise, New Cross, on the 40th anniversary of what is now called 'The Battle of Lewisham'. In October 2019 this mural was installed on the wall of Goldsmith's University Library, facing onto Lewisham Way in New Cross. The mural was created in partnership with community workshops and designer Ted Low, a Goldsmiths graduate.

ASQUITH GIBBES

RACE EQUALITY CAMPAIGNER (1934–2013)
Lewisham Police Station, 43 Lewisham High Street, SE13 5JZ

Asquith Gibbes was born in Grenada and moved to London in the 1950s. He was the first Principal Racial Equality Officer, managing the then Council for Community Relations. Also, as part of an independent advisory group on race, he liaised with the police on stop and search (SUS) methods. In 1993 he led the group that created the Kick Racism out of Football campaign at Millwall FC. Gibbes also served as a governor at Lewisham College and started the Student Voice empowerment programme that went nationwide. In 2009 he was awarded an MBE in recognition of over 30 years of service with community groups, schools and the police. An annual Asquith Gibbes award is given by Lewisham police to recognise those who continue to promote racial equality and social cohesion within the borough.

This memorial to Asquith Gibbes was unveiled at Lewisham police station in June 2019. Attendees included family, friends and colleagues as well as the current Mayor of Lewisham. The black stone memorial features a map of the borough in white marble with a portrait of Gibbes at the centre. It was created by local stone-carver Simon Smith.

THE BROCKLEY BARGE PUB

PUBLIC HOUSE
184 Brockley Road, Brockley, SE4 2RR

See Bob Marley, p. 95.

STEPHEN LAWRENCE CENTRE

COMMUNITY CENTRE
Brookmill Road, Deptford, SE8 4HU

See Stephen Lawrence p. 169.

BLUE EARTH

SCULPTURE
The Horniman Museum, 100 London Road, Forest Hill, SE23 3PQ

The rotating globe *Blue Earth 1807–2007* was unveiled in December 2007 as a major new permanent addition to the Horniman Museum's World Gallery. The sculpture was created by British-born artist Taslim Martin, and commemorated the 1807 abolition of transatlantic enslavement.

The transatlantic slave routes have been etched into the stone, tracing Britain's triangular slave trade. These include the main shipping routes of Liverpool, Bristol and London to West Africa, as well as charting the journey from Africa to North America, the Caribbean and South America. The sphere measures 1.2 metres (4ft) in diameter. Visitors are encouraged to engage with *Blue Earth* by rotating it to view the connecting trade routes across the world. Martin's sculpture conveys the impact the African diaspora has had across the world and aims to help people to understand its legacy, which continues to impact on numerous countries today. In 1997 he was awarded the Sir Eduardo Paolozzi Travel Scholarship, which he used to facilitate research into West African sculpture.

THE MIGRATION MUSEUM

MUSEUM
Lewisham Shopping Centre, SE13 7HB

The Migration Museum explores the movement of people to and from Britain and how this has formed the identity of the nation. Formerly located in Lambeth, it is now situated in Lewisham shopping centre. The museum holds events, exhibitions and educational workshops. Past exhibitions are also accessible on the museum's online gallery, which includes the photography collection: '100 Images of Migration'.

GREENWICH PARK

FORMER SITE OF MONTAGU HOUSE
Junction of Charlton Way and Chesterfield Gate, SE3 7AP

A memorial plaque to Ignatus Sancho (see p. 34) can be seen on the wall of Greenwich Park, at the junction of Charlton Way and Chesterfield Walk. This is the former site of Montagu House, demolished in 1815, home to the Duke of Montagu who had taught Sancho how to read.

FURTHER AFIELD

BLACK LIVES MATTER

MURAL (2020)
General Gordon Square, Woolwich, SE18 6FH

In 2020 the words 'Black Lives Matter' were painted in giant yellow letters across General Gordon Square in central Woolwich in a show of support for the equality movement. The lettering spans the length of the walkway from Thomas Street to General Gordon Place. It was unveiled by the Greenwich Council leader and attendees included a number of the borough's faith leaders. The artwork is the result of collaboration between the council and the Runnymede Trust, an independent race equality think-tank established in 1968.

Black Lives Matter (BLM) was founded in the USA in 2013 and is now a global organisation. It was created in response to the murder of teenager Trayvon Martin in 2012 and the acquittal of his killer. In May 2020 the video of George Floyd's killing by a police officer sparked worldwide shock, protest and demonstrations. Statues of prominent white figures involved in the slave trade in the USA, Europe and the UK were pulled down or defaced. BLM signs have been painted in cities across America, including in front of Donald Trump's business organisation Trump Tower in New York. In Bristol the statue of the Royal African Company member and slave trader Edward Colston was toppled. It was temporarily replaced by a statue of a black female protester. In the UK there has been a seismic shift and a positive movement for black representation, structural change and equality across the board.

IRA ALDRIDGE

SHAKESPEARIAN ACTOR (1807–67)

5 Hamlet Road, Upper Norwood, SE19 2AP

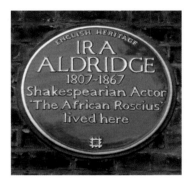

Ira Aldridge was born in America but came to London as a young man to pursue acting. He made his West End debut in 1825 and, despite the prejudice he faced, his run was extended, and he was named the 'African Roscius' in tribute to the ancient Roman actor. Aldridge toured the provinces and in 1833 played Othello at the Covent Garden Theatre. It was the first time a black actor had performed this role on a West End stage. It was also the year when the bill to abolish slavery was passing through Parliament. The theatre cancelled his engagement after two performances due to pressure from the critics.

Aldridge toured England and Europe and is credited with taking Shakespeare to Poland and Russia. He made a triumphant return to the London stage in 1848. Settling in London, he became a naturalised British citizen in 1863, but died in 1867 while touring in Poland. He is buried in the town of Lodz, Poland. His daughter Amanda worked with

the African American actor Paul Robeson (see p. 108) on his voice and diction. Almost a century later, in 1930, Robeson was the second black actor to play Othello in London.

This English Heritage plaque was unveiled in 2007.

CRYSTAL PALACE PARK SPHINXES
MONUMENT (1852)
Crystal Palace Park grounds, SE19 2GA

The six Grade-II-listed sphinxes in the Crystal Palace Park grounds were once 'gatekeepers' to Joseph Paxton's Crystal Palace, which housed the Great Exhibition of 1851 in Hyde Park. In 1852 they were relocated to the new Crystal Palace Park. The glass palace was destroyed by a fire in 1936. The sphinxes are set in pairs and positioned on the grand Italian terraces, at the head of the granite steps. The mythical creatures, with the head of a human and body of a lion, are decorated with hieroglyphs. They were thought to be copied from an original red granite Egyptian sphinx in the Louvre, Paris. Originating from Egypt, North Africa, the sphinxes, like the Great Sphinx of Giza on the west bank of the Nile, are important monumental statues.

In 2016 the sphinxes underwent extensive conservation work and repair. Their repainting was the final stage in returning them to their former glory, as they would have been painted red repeatedly until the 1900s. The specialist terracotta mineral paint will conserve and protect the concrete structures from future decay for generations to come.

SAMUEL COLERIDGE-TAYLOR

MUSICIAN AND COMPOSER (1875–1912)

66 Charles Street, Croyden, CR0 1SG

Samuel Coleridge-Taylor was born in Holborn in 1875 to Alice Martin, an English woman, and Dr Daniel Taylor from Sierra Leone. He studied the violin and piano at the Royal College of Music as well as music composition. He also taught and worked as a professor at the Crystal Palace School of Music and conducted the orchestra at the Croydon Conservatoire. In 1899 he married Jessie Walmsley, with whom he had a son, named Hiawatha, and a daughter, Gwendolyn. Later, Gwendolyn took the name Avril and became a conductor-composer in her own right.

Taylor wrote his most famous composition, *Hiawatha's Wedding Feast*, between 1898 and 1900. This referenced the native American hero Hiawatha, and the introduction fuses classical music with the African American spiritual song 'Nobody Knows the Trouble I've Seen'. Although it was commercially successful, Taylor had sold the rights to the music and did not benefit from it.

In 1900 Taylor was a leading delegate at the first Pan-African Conference in London alongside John Archer, African American W. E. B. Du Bois, the US civil rights leader, and Henry Sylvester William. During his life he toured the US, published over a hundred works and sought to elevate black music, from his folk collection of *Twenty-Four Negro Melodies* in 1905 to the *Othello Suite* in 1909. The preface to the *Melodies* was written by Booker T. Washington, a prominent educator, author and spokesman for African Americans.

Taylor was only 37 when he died suddenly of pneumonia in 1912. There was a national outpouring of grief, with crowds attending his funeral. In the same year, a memorial concert was organised for him at the Royal Albert Hall, with proceeds going to his family. Many were concerned that he had received no royalties and profited little from his works. His case led to the establishment of the Performing Rights Society. Coleridge-Taylor is buried in Bandon Hill Cemetery, Wallington, Surrey. From 1924 to 1939 the Royal Albert Hall held an annual Hiawatha Season of large-scale performances.

This steel portrait bench statue of Samuel Coleridge-Taylor was erected in 2013 by the charity group Sustrans, which has unveiled a series of community figures throughout the UK. Coleridge-Taylor is one of a set of three, the other two being Dame Flora Robson and Ronnie Corbett. He also has a Greater London Council plaque at 30 Dagnall Park in South Norwood and a Nubian Jak plaque at St Leonard's Road, Croydon, in celebration of his centenary in 2012.

FURTHER INFORMATION

Plaques and Memorials
www.english-heritage.org.uk | www.londonremembers.com
www.nubianjak.org \www.BlackPlaqueProject.com

Timelines
The Black Presence in Britain
www.blackpresence.co.uk/black-british-timeline/

Our Migration Story 1750–1900
www.ourmigrationstory.org.uk

Passage to Freedom
www.royalparks.org.uk/__data/assets/pdf_file/0011/41510/
passagetofreedomteacherspack1.pdf

Timeline of the British Empire
www.historic-uk.com/HistoryUK/HistoryofBritain/Timeline-Of-The-
British-Empire/

Timeline of the Slave Trade and Abolition
www.historicengland.org.uk/research/inclusive-heritage/the-slave-
trade-and-abolition/time-line/

Legacy of British Slave Ownership
www.ucl.ac.uk/lbs/

Black History
100 Great Black Britons
www.100greatblackbritons.com

The Black Curriculum – a social enterprise founded in 2019 to address
the lack of black British history in the UK curriculum
www.theblackcurriculum.com

British Library – Black Britain and Andrea Levy archives
www.bl.uk/collection-guides/black-britain-publications

The Equiano Society
Formed in 1996 to publicise and celebrate the life and work of Olaudah Equiano. www.equiano.uk/the-equiano-society/

George Ryan documents
www.nationalarchives.gov.uk/pathways/blackhistory/journeys/virtual_tour_html/londondocs/muster.htm

Goldsmiths University
MA courses in: Black History, Black British Writing and Race, Media and Social Justice.
www.gold.ac.uk/pg/ma-black-british-history

John Blanke documents
www.nationalarchives.gov.uk/pathways/blackhistory/early_times/blanke.htm

National Archives – Black History
www.nationalarchives.gov.uk/pathways/blackhistory/

SOAS University (School of Oriental and African Studies)
BA in African Studies. www.soas.ac.uk

FURTHER READING

Non-fiction History

- *100 Great Black Britons* (2020) by Patrick Vernon and Angelina Osborne

- *Belle: The True Story of Dido Belle* (2014) by Paula Byrne

- *Black and British: A Forgotten History* (2018) by David Olusoga

- *Black Londoners 1880–1990* (2009) by Susan Okokon.

- *Black Poppies* (2014) by Stephen Bourne

- *Black Tudors* (2017) by Miranda Kaufmann

- *Blackamoores* (2013) by Onyeka Nubia

- *Brit(ish): On Race, Identity and Belonging* (2018) by Afua Hirsch

- *Doing Nothing Is Not an Option: The Radical Lives of Eric and Jessica Huntley* (2014) by Margaret Andrews

- *Homecoming: Voices of the Windrush Generation* (2019) by Colin Grant

- *How Europe Underdeveloped Africa* (1972) by Walter Rodney

- *A Kick in the Belly: Women, Slavery & Resistance* (2020) by Stella Dadzie

- *Mother Country: Real Stories of the Windrush Children* (2018) edited by Charlie Brinkhurst-Cuff

- *Natives: Race and Class in the Ruins of Empire* (2019) by Akala

- *Staying Power: The History of Black People in Britain* (1984) by Peter Fryer

- *The Windrush Betrayal: Exposing the Hostile Environment* (2019) by Amelia Gentleman

Art & Culture
- *Black Artists in British Art: A History Since the 1950s* (2014) by Eddie Chambers

- *Meet the Artist: Frank Bowling* (2019) by Zoe Whitley

- *Sounds Like London: 100 Years of Black Music in the Capital* (2013) by Lloyd Bradley

Fiction
- *The Book of Echoes* (2020) by Rosanna Amaka

- *Girl, Woman, Other* (2019) by Bernardine Evaristo

- *Incomparable World* (1996) by S. I. Martin

- *The Lonely Londoners* (1956) by Samuel Selvon

- *Second-Class Citizen* (1974) by Buchi Emecheta

- *Small Island* (2004)/The Long Song (2010) by Andrea Levy

- *Surge by Jay Bernard* (2019)

- *Things Fall Apart* (1958) by Chinua Achebe

- *White Teeth* (2000) by Zadie Smith

Books for Children and Young Adults

Black History/non-fiction

– *Black and British: A Short, Essential History* (2020) by David Olusoga

– *Black History Matters* (2019) by Robin Walker

– *'I Will Not Be Erased': Our Stories about Growing Up as People of Colour* (2019) by gal-dem

– *Our Roots: Black History Sketchbook* (2004) by Tayo Fatunla

– *Walter Tull: Footballer, Soldier, Hero* (2011) by Dan Lyndon

– *Young, Gifted and Black* (2019) by Jamia Wilson

– *Coming to England* (2016) by Floella Benjamin

Fiction

– *Cane Warriors* (2020) by Alex Wheatle

– *Diver's Daughter: A Tudor Story* (2019) by Patrice Lawrence

– *Freedom* (2018) by Catherine Johnson

– *Noughts and Crosses* (2001) by Malorie Blackman

– *The Story of the Windrush* (2018) by K. N. Chimbiri

– *Windrush Child* (2020) by Benjamin Zephaniah

Other

– Art UK: Explore an online selection of art and stories including black artists, history and legacies. www.artuk.org/

– Victoria and Albert Museum: Holds a collection of African and Caribbean artefacts and artworks including an 1802 print of Toussaint L'Ouverture. They also offer tours and online trails including 'Britain and the Caribbean' and 'Africans in Europe'.

– Windrush Foundation: A registered charity that designs and delivers heritage projects. www.windrushfoundation.com/

INDEX

CREDITS

All photos are © of the authors, unless listed: 8 Steve Eason / Wikimedia Commons; 13 Martin Luther King: Uncle Leo / Shutterstock.com; Nelson Mandela: bamrung isarakul / Shutterstock.com; 25 Daniel Rossi Limpi / Shutterstock.com; 33 Jono Photography / Shutterstock.com; 39 Emma Wesley / National Portrait Gallery London; 42 Simon Harriyott / Wikimedia Commons; 45 Michael De Leon, 2015; 47 chrisdorney / Shutterstock.com; 53 fritz16 / Shutterstock.com; 54 Sue Martin / Shutterstock.com; 88 Spudgun67, CC BY-SA 4.0 / Wikimedia Commons; 93 Toby Laurent-Belson / Avril Nanton; 94 John Gaffen 2 / Alamy Stock Photo; 96 Image courtesy of Nubian Jak copyright © 2020; 97 Spudgun67, CC BY-SA 4.0 / Wikimedia Commons; 126 Stamp designs © Royal Mail Group Limited; 166 College of Arms MS Westminster Tournament Roll, 1511. Reproduced by permission of the Kings, Heralds and Pursuivants of Arms.

Every effort has been made to trace the copyright holders and we apologise in advance for any unintentional omissions or errors. We would be pleased to apply corrections in following editions of this publication.

ACKNOWLEDGMENTS

My wonderful husband, Desmond Holloway, for all his support; my mentor Robin Walker; supportive friends Pauline Mullings, Claire Adeyemi, Veronica Bignall, Elspeth McKay and Mensah Sesay who helped me along the way. Avril

Thanks to my mother, Nellie Burton; family and friends Cynthia Ravagnan, Joy Baker and Sandra Reynolds for their encouragement on this journey; and also Edem Selormey and everyone at Southwark libraries. Jody

Thanks to Helen Brocklehurst and the team at Fox Chapel Publishers for making our project happen.